KIDS CARE!

75 ways to **make a difference** for people, animals & the environment

Rebecca Olien

Illustrations by Michael Kline

williamsonbooks™

Nashville, Tennessee

ISBN-13: 978-0-8249-6793-2 (hardcover)
ISBN-13: 978-0-8249-6792-5 (softcover)

Published by Williamson Books
An imprint of Ideals Publications
A Guideposts Company
535 Metroplex Drive, Suite 250
Nashville, Tennessee 37211
www.idealsbooks.com

Library of Congress Cataloging-in-Publication Data
Olien, Rebecca.
  Kids care! : 75 ways to make a difference for people, animals & the
environment / Rebecca Olien ; illustrations by Michael Kline.
     p. cm. — (A Williamson kids can! book)
  Includes bibliographical references and index.
  ISBN-13: 978-0-8249-6793-2 (case : alk. paper)
  ISBN-13: 978-0-8249-6792-5 (pbk. : alk. paper)
  1. Caring—Juvenile literature. I. Kline, Michael P. II. Title.
  BJ1475.O45 2007
  177'.7—dc22   2006036186

Project editor: **Emily Stetson**
Interior design: **Linda Williamson, Dawson Design**
Interior Illustrations: **Michael Kline**
Cover design and illustrations: **Michael Kline**

Printed and bound in China

10 9 8 7 6 5 4 3 2 1

Dedication
*To the creative and caring
spirits in all of us. No matter
what age, let us all strive to
protect the planet and share
our talents to make the
world a kinder place.*

Permissions
Permission is granted by Williamson Books and Ideals Publications to use limited material or suggestions previously
published in the following titles: on pages 14, 92, 97, 105, from *Boredom Busters!* by Avery Hart and Paul Mantell; on
pages 64, 70, 74, 79, 102, from *Kids' Easy-to-Create Wildlife Habitats* by Emily Stetson; on pages 12–13, from *The
Kids' Guide to Making Scrapbooks & Photo Albums* by Laura Check; on page 9, from *The Little Hands Playtime! Book*
by Regina Curtis; on page 24, from *Make Your Own Christmas Ornaments* by Ginger Johnson; on page 9, from
Summer Fun! by Susan Williamson.

CONTENTS

KIDS CAN MAKE A DIFFERENCE!

All around us there is a need for caring. We hear, see, and read about homeless people and families who go to bed hungry. Wild animals need people to safeguard their habitats, while household pets need playtime and attention to keep them active and healthy. Add to that the news of shrinking rain forests, polluted water and air, and the strain on Mother Earth's natural bounty, and it's clear there are many areas that would benefit from caring kids like you.

Sometimes the need seems overwhelming, and some kids might feel too small or young to really help. But you *can* help, every day, in little and big ways. **This book shows you how, with more than 75 simple ways that you can make a difference, starting right now.** You'll find ideas for making helpful crafts, pet toys, and meaningful gifts for people in need in your community; there are action-packed ideas for helping wildlife near and far, and suggestions on how you can help conserve the earth's resources. You can start close to home, or reach out to those in need all over the globe. Try activities on your own or combine your efforts with others. Look for the KIDS CARE TOGETHER icon that highlights activities perfect for a group.

Whatever activity you choose, you'll find that caring is contagious. Your enthusiasm and helpful attitude will attract others who also want to make a difference. And with more helping hands, you'll have even more creative fun and make a bigger difference. Way to go! Because you care, you'll make the world a better place for us all.

KIDS CARE ABOUT PEOPLE

How do you show you care? It's easy — there are so many ways! Caring for other people is something you do in the best of times and the could-be-better times, when there is an abundance of joyfulness, and when everything seems difficult. All of us from time to time need someone to help us, and all of us have opportunities — every day — to help others in need.

Showing you care can be as simple as saying hello to someone who is new in town, or waving to an acquaintance, friend, or neighbor. It is shoveling the snow from a neighbor's walk without being asked or helping someone bring the trash curbside. When you listen to someone who seems extra-quiet or sit with someone who is alone in the school cafeteria, you are sending welcome signals of caring that anyone can do. Caring is about actions you do for others that come from your heart. You can show you care by making homemade cards and welcoming gifts, by organizing a food drive or going on a hike for the hungry, and — most important — by making time for others.

Everywhere you go, there are people who can benefit from the kindness of kids. And by helping others and being sensitive to what is going on in the lives of others, you help yourself by knowing that you really *can* make a difference.

·LISTENING·WITH·CARE·

Listening is one of the most important things you can do to show you care. Listening is different from hearing: when you listen, you find the meaning from the speaker's words and the tone of voice used. If you can see the speaker, you get more listening clues from the speaker's body language (how he sits or stands, fidgets, and holds his arms and hands).

You can help someone turn a not-so-great day or a lonely day into a really good day, just by listening. And you can help someone celebrate an accomplishment by listening as she talks excitedly about what she did. When people share their experiences, concerns, joys, and ideas with you, they are sharing who they are and what is important to them. Listening lets them know *you* think who they are and what they have to say is important, too!

Interview Someone Special

For a formal interview, have some preplanned questions with you as well as a notebook and perhaps a digital recorder. For a less formal meeting or conversation, be prepared to interact with and respond to the speaker. Use these same listening skills when you are simply talking with someone, too. Everyone benefits when you share the gift of listening.

What you need

- Notebook and pencil (optional)
- Tape or digital recorder (optional)
- Camera, film or digital (optional)

1 Choose a person to interview (an elderly friend, a neighbor, or a special pal). Arrange some time to spend together.

2 Ask the person questions—an older person or someone from another part of the world might like to tell you about his school days, for instance. (See QUESTIONS, QUESTIONS below for more ideas.) Encourage the speaker by asking questions and being an attentive listener (see LISTENING TIPS, page 8). Ask questions that help you learn details about the feelings involved at that time. Listening is simply one half of a good conversation—and the more you listen, the more you are apt to want to know!

3 If you would like to record the wonderful stories people tell you, be sure to get permission from each person beforehand. You'll be amazed at what you hear when you replay your interview. A good listener can discover a lot just from the tone of someone's voice. Did you find out more by listening a second time?

Questions, Questions

Write a list of questions ahead of time to use as a guide for your interview or special conversation. Here are some questions you might like to ask:

? Where is the most beautiful place you have been? What made it beautiful to you?

? Who has made a big difference in your life?

? What is one of the silliest things you have seen?

? Did curiosity ever get you into trouble?

? What is something you did that you are proud of?

? Share about a time when you solved a difficult problem.

? Describe one of the most surprising things you have experienced.

? What is one of the most creative things you have ever made or done?

? What is your favorite holiday, and what makes it so special?

No way!

And then what happened?

Really?

That's So Cool!

· LISTENING TIPS ·

Being a good listener takes practice. We enjoy sharing *our* experiences so much that sometimes it is difficult to remember to listen while others are talking! Here are a few tips on being a good listener:

• **Listen with enthusiasm.** No one likes to talk to someone who looks bored.

• **Look at the person** who is talking. Make eye contact and give signals such as nods and smiles to let him or her know you are listening.

• **Pay full attention** to what the speaker is saying. Focus on the conversation. Try not to think about something else or plan what you want to say next. To be a good listener, forget about yourself and your surroundings and concentrate on what the person you are talking with is saying.

• **Don't interrupt.** Wait until the speaker is finished talking before sharing your own experiences.

• **Ask questions** to help the speaker share more details about what happened, how she felt, and how she feels now about events in her life (see QUESTIONS, QUESTIONS, page 7, for ideas).

• **Be patient.** Give the speaker plenty of time to think about what he is going to say. Sometimes it takes awhile to think of an answer to a question. Good listeners don't rush the speaker.

• **Repeat some things** the speaker tells you to make sure you understand. For instance, you might say, "Wow! The bear was heading right toward you, so you had to make a difficult choice."

MORE FUN! Make a "retelling" book

Ask permission from each speaker to collect a few of the stories from your interviews for a book. The book can hold several stories from one speaker or stories from several different speakers. Add illustrations or photos (with the speaker's permission) to each story. You can also record a retelling of a story or an interview to use with SOUND OFF FOR FUN! (see page 14). Give a copy of the book (or show) as a special gift to anyone who shared a story with you.

Safe Speaking Zone

What about when you are the one who is having an "off" day and needs a good listener? Sometimes you may not even want to talk about what you are feeling. That's just fine! The important thing to know is that if you *do* have something on your mind, you can always tell someone you trust about it. Think about the people you can talk to if something is bothering you. Isn't it nice to know that people care?

ACTS OF CARING

Lend a friendly ear

Listening can happen any time of day (or night!) and anywhere. You don't need a special place or an appointment to be a great listener. If you have a friend who seems extra-quiet or upset, spend some special one-on-one time with him, being a good listener. Be *present* (that means "be attentive") to whatever he has to say. If your friend doesn't want to talk, don't be offended. Instead, just sit quietly together, listen to some music, read together, or play a board game or a card game. The most important thing is that your friend knows you care — which is clear because you are there, listening!

• SAYING • "YOU'RE • SPECIAL!" •

There are plenty of good ideas on these pages for things to make that are certain to cheer someone up. If you have a friend or classmate who is housebound but who can still have company, then perhaps you can arrange with a group of classmates to take turns visiting a few times a week. Those visits will be something your friend in need will never forget! Making a special effort is another way to say that you care.

Caring Cards

Cards are a great way to send someone the message that you care. They can be sent any time of year to anyone needing encouragement, congratulations, or cheering up, or simply as a way to share a special thought. Whatever the reason, your own homemade card made on recycled paper (see page 12) is sure to brighten someone's day.

What you need

- Scissors
- Paper (to make your own, see page 12)
- Old magazines, for cutting
- Glue
- Tempera paints and paintbrushes
- Photos (optional)
- Pens, markers, colored pencils
- Card-sized envelope (available from office supply stores, or make your own)
- Postage stamp (if mailing the card)

1 Cut and fold the paper to fit inside the envelopes.

2 Decide on a purpose for your card and who you will send it to. Think about what that person likes. Do you want your card to be silly, serious, or somewhere in between?

3 Choose the materials to make your card. You can decorate the front, inside, and back of the card, or just the front.

❤ Make collage cards by cutting out pictures and words from old magazines and gluing them onto the card in a fun arrangement.

❤ Paint a picture and glue it to the card.

❤ Use a photograph as a picture for the front or inside.

❤ Draw with markers, colored pencils, or ink.

4 Choose a message for inside the card. Use your own words, write a poem, choose a favorite quotation, or write a joke.

5 Address, stamp (if mailing), and hand deliver or mail your card! (If mailing your card, it's a good idea to check the postage, because the materials you use may make the card weigh more than a usual store-bought card. The folks at the post office will be happy to make sure your card has the right amount of postage.)

Handmade Papers from Recycled Print!

Making paper is actually easier to do than it is to describe, so don't let the instructions overwhelm you! The papers you make will be well worth this small effort and will make your cards seem like very special gifts for someone.

What you need

- Paper scraps, all kinds, from recycle bin
- Water
- Sparkles, ribbon bits, scraps of colorful paper, flower petals (optional)
- Blender (with adult permission)
- Piece of screening or netting, hot-glued to an old picture frame or in an embroidery hoop
- Dishpan
- Old towels, 2
- Piece of old sheet
- Sponge
- Rolling pin, or substitute
- Dull table knife

1 Soak paper scraps in warm water for 30 minutes or overnight. Add some sparkles, pieces of ribbon, scraps of colored paper, or some flower petals, if you want.

2 With adult permission, fill a blender half full of water and add a handful of the soaked paper mixture; blend until you have a souplike mush, called *pulp*.

Use me with permission!

3 To make the paper, lay the framed screening or netting in the bottom of a dishpan and fill with about 3″ (7.5 cm) of water. Add the pulp. Slowly slide the screen back and forth through the pulpy mixture, then lift it straight up, so that the pulp is evenly distributed on the screen.

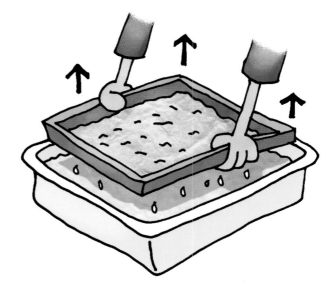

4 Set the screen over the dishpan and let it drain. When no more water is dripping, place the screen on a towel. Lay a piece of an old sheet on top of the pulp and gently press with a sponge to remove the excess water. Turn the screen and sheet over, letting the paper fall onto the sheet. Cover with a dry towel and use a rolling pin to squeeze out more water (this strengthens the paper, too).

5 Let the paper dry overnight. Then carefully peel it from the sheet using a table knife. *Ta-da* — recycled paper for a homemade card!

Little acts of kindness

There are lots of little ways you can show you care that don't need any materials at all. Smiling at someone at school or talking with someone is always nice to do. Include a person who looks left out into your group at lunch, or offer to help someone with his homework — then watch for that glimmer of a smile! Imagine how *you* would want to be included or helped, and you'll think of lots of other ways, too.

Show caring at home by making your bed, keeping your room neat, washing the dishes, preparing your lunch for school, taking out the garbage, playing with a younger sibling, and taking care of the family pet. If you don't think of these as chores but, rather, consider them daily acts of kindness, you might actually enjoy doing some of these things! By helping out, you are making it easier for someone else to have a more relaxed day. To top it off, how about leaving your mom or dad a nice note? Put it where they'll be sure to find it, like on their pillow or taped to the fridge. Letting them know you love them is one of the best gifts a kid can give!

Sound Off for Fun!

Put together an old-fashioned radio show full of stories, music, and humor. Share your show with friends and family members, or with anyone who would enjoy a little added fun. Be sure to invite people of all ages, because everyone will enjoy your thoughtfulness!

What you need

- Tape recorder or digital recorder
- Tape or other recording medium
- Microphone

(Or, use a computer, recording software, and a compact disc if you have access to them.)

1 Collect material for your show. You might like to listen to some old recordings of radio shows for ideas. You can tell jokes, read stories, sing songs, play an instrument, and talk about interesting events or projects. Choose material that you think your listeners would enjoy.

2 If someone is ill and missing school or team practices, make a recording of messages from classmates and teammates.

3 Practice your pieces. Decide on an order for your material. Record!

4 Make a tape or CD of your recording to give for a great "caring surprise."

Put On a Talent Show

Use lots of kids' talents for a "live" show with a wider range of material. Take turns performing. Use your show to help raise money for people in need, such as for a relief organization or for your local food shelf. Create lyrics and music about your causes, too! Who knows? Your group may have so much fun you may decide to do a holiday special! And don't forget to sell some popcorn to add to your fund-raising efforts! (For more details on fund-raising basics, see pages 120 to 123.)

Boredom Buster Box

Have you ever been sick, broken a leg, or had such bad allergies you couldn't go outside? One of the hardest things kids and adults have to deal with when they have an injury or illness is not being able to participate in activities they are accustomed to doing. Giving someone who has to stay quiet a BOREDOM BUSTER BOX full of games, puzzles, and surprises can be a big help in making the time pass more quickly, and it shows you care — the greatest gift of all!

1 Decorate the box with paint and markers, or glue on paper cutouts. Print "Boredom Buster Box" on the box in big letters. This box will keep all of the activities and treats together.

2 Choose items to make for your box (see BORDOM BUSTERS! for ideas) and add any of your own wonderful ideas! Think about what the recipient enjoys doing, so that your gift will really help him or her to pass the time away.

what you need

- Cardboard box
- Tempera paints and paintbrushes
- Markers
- Construction paper, various colors
- Scissors
- Glue
- Items to include in the box (see page 17 for ideas)

3 Include items in the BOREDOM BUSTER BOX to help kids create, such as a glue stick, rounded scissors (pointed scissors are dangerous in bed!), drawing paper, and crayons.

4 Add an extra surprise, such as an inexpensive deck of cards or a bottle of bubbles, and wrap it up with a funny note. It's sure to bring a smile!

Boredom Busters!

Mazes

Draw pathways every which way, providing lots of choices and dead ends. Make sure one path continues to the end! Mazes can be made in the shapes of animals, buildings, rockets, or anything you choose.

Word searches, crossword puzzles, word scrambles

Make your own word games based on themes you think the recipient would enjoy. Graph paper makes these games easier to create by placing letters in evenly arranged squares.

Cartoons

Draw funny characters doing silly things, or tell a funny story through your drawings. Add speech balloons or write jokes under your cartoons.

Dot-to-dot

Make a mystery picture solved by connecting dots in order. First, draw a picture with black marker (or find a picture to trace). Place a piece of paper on top and place dots along the lines of your drawing. Number the dots in order.

Puppet in a bag

Cut shapes from colored sticker paper (the kind used to make labels); also cut shapes from colored paper and place in a paper lunch bag along with a glue stick. Provide drawings or a sample paper-bag puppet for ideas to help the person get started.

Story characters

Make fun or mysterious story characters from cardboard or heavy paper. How about a dragon, alien, extremely tall person, very tiny whale, or a great big fish? Glue characters on craft sticks to use for handles. Put inside an envelope and label "Once Upon a Time." These are great for pretending or as ideas for writing a story. They can also be used with a flashlight to make shadow puppets on the wall.

Help Kids in Crisis

A BOREDOM BUSTER BOX (see page 16) is great for kids who are away from home because of family circumstances (or temporarily without a home). Ask a group of friends to make several boxes to bring to homeless shelters and crisis centers (call ahead so that you make enough boxes for each child at the shelter or center to have her own). Leave a place for the child's name on each BOREDOM BUSTER BOX, so that he knows it was made specifically for him. Include a separate personal note to each child so that each kid knows someone cares. (For more ideas on helping needy kids and families, see page 25.)

TRY THIS!

For Adults, Too!

Adults who are sick or can't get out much will appreciate the thoughtfulness of a personalized box as well.
Is there an older person who can't easily leave the house who lives on your block or in your neighborhood? Someone who is confined to a wheelchair or who is ill? Adults would enjoy drawings and other art created by you. Add your own cartoons, make word searches harder with more words, cut crosswords from the newspaper, and add lots of art! Adults love visits from children, too, if you have permission to visit.

Think of what else that person might enjoy. Perhaps some fresh fruit? Home-baked muffins? A jar of homemade jam? Include a card you designed at home (see CARING CARDS, page 10). Then deliver your BOREDOM BUSTER BOX with a smile!

A Welcome Kit

Have you ever been the new kid at school? It can be overwhelming to find your way around a strange town, and to locate your locker and classes in an unfamiliar school. You may wonder if kids will be nice to you and whether you will find friends and "fit in." Help someone new to school and to the neighborhood by making a "welcoming" kit full of helpful information.

What you need

- School and neighborhood maps
- Paper
- Pencil
- Markers
- Cloth bag (Design and make your own! See Bag It!, page 94.)
- Stickers or other decorative items (optional)
- A small gift such as school decals, either made by you or store-bought

1 Collect information helpful to a new person at school or in town. You might include:

⊚ School and neighborhood maps (ask in the school office or town hall, or draw your own version) ⊚ City map of the closest town ⊚ List of neighborhood or town information (library hours, town gatherings or traditions, kids' organizations such as Scouts or the "Y") ⊚ List of teachers and staff ⊚ Class list ⊚ Bus route information ⊚ Directions to the closest park or outdoor recreation area ⊚ Directions for getting lunch (and an invitation to sit with you at your table!) ⊚ Stickers for notebooks ⊚ Colorful pencil ⊚ Decorated name tag for desk or locker ⊚ Fun-shaped eraser ⊚ "Welcome to School" card signed by classmates (see CARING CARDS, page 10)

2 Place all items in a bag decorated with your school name, logo, and other drawings.

3 Share the bag and its contents with the new student. Offer to give a school tour and explain how things work at your school. Maybe you can even arrange to accompany the new student on her first bus ride.

Baby Blanket

This blanket will be a welcome gift to anyone who is expecting a new member of the family. Make a blanket for an organization that supports new parents, give your blanket to the newborn nursery of the hospital for a gift to a needy family, or donate your blanket to an organization that helps families find housing, such as a refugee relief group or a family shelter. A family who is having a difficult time will appreciate your thoughtfulness as they tuck their baby in for a nap.

What you need

- Black crayon
- Drawing paper
- White or light-colored fleece fabric, 1 yard (1 m)
- Iron (use with adult help)
- Nontoxic fabric paints or markers

1 With the black crayon, draw big outlines of animals, smiling faces, flowers, stars, and hearts on drawing paper. Press hard with the crayon and use thick lines.

2 Create enough pictures so they fill the space of the fabric. (Nine large pictures, one in each square foot (30 cm) of fabric, is a good fit.)

3 Have an adult turn your pictures *facedown* on the fabric and gently iron over them. The crayon will leave outlines on the fabric.

4 Use nontoxic fabric paints or markers to color in your animals and other designs.

Teddy Bear Care

A stuffed toy is a comforting companion to children everywhere. Share stuffed bears you make not only with children you know personally, but also with hospitals, disaster-relief organizations, refugee-help organizations, local shelters, and volunteer agencies (see page 123 for a list of groups you might consider helping).

What you need

- Pencil
- Paper bag
- Tracing paper (optional)
- Craft scissors
- Soft fuzzy fabric, 7" x 14" (17.5 x 35 cm) for a small bear; ½ yard (.5 m) for a larger bear or several small bears
- Fabric marker
- Pins
- Fabric scissors
- Needle and thread, or sewing machine (for use with adult help)
- Batting or cotton balls, for stuffing
- Felt scraps and fabric glue, or fabric paints

1 Draw a bear shape on the paper bag, or, if you like, you can trace the TEDDY BEAR TEMPLATE (page 23) onto tracing paper. Cut out the paper-bag bear or traced template to use as a pattern.

2 Fold the fabric in half, with the furry sides together (on the inside). Place the pattern on the fabric and carefully draw around the pattern with a fabric marker.

3 Remove the pattern. Pin the fabric pieces together inside the marker line. Cut the pieces out.

4 Thread the needle and knot the ends. With the two bear pieces still pinned, sew around the edges of the bear with a running stitch (see TAKE A STITCH, page 24), ¼" (5 mm) from the outer edge of the fabric, leaving a small opening on one side as shown. Make your sewing strong, with small stitches placed close together. Or, have an adult help you stitch the bear on a sewing machine. Knot and snip the thread; remove the pins.

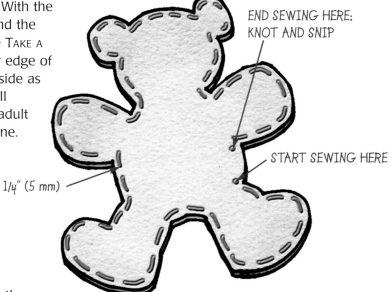

END SEWING HERE; KNOT AND SNIP

START SEWING HERE

1/4" (5 mm)

5 Turn the bear right side out by pulling the fabric through the unstitched opening. Use a pencil to push out the fabric in the legs, feet, arms, and ears.

6 Fill the bear with stuffing, then sew the opening together using the whipstitch (see page 24).

7 Cut out a nose, eyes, mouth, and other features from felt and glue in place, or use fabric paint to decorate your bear.

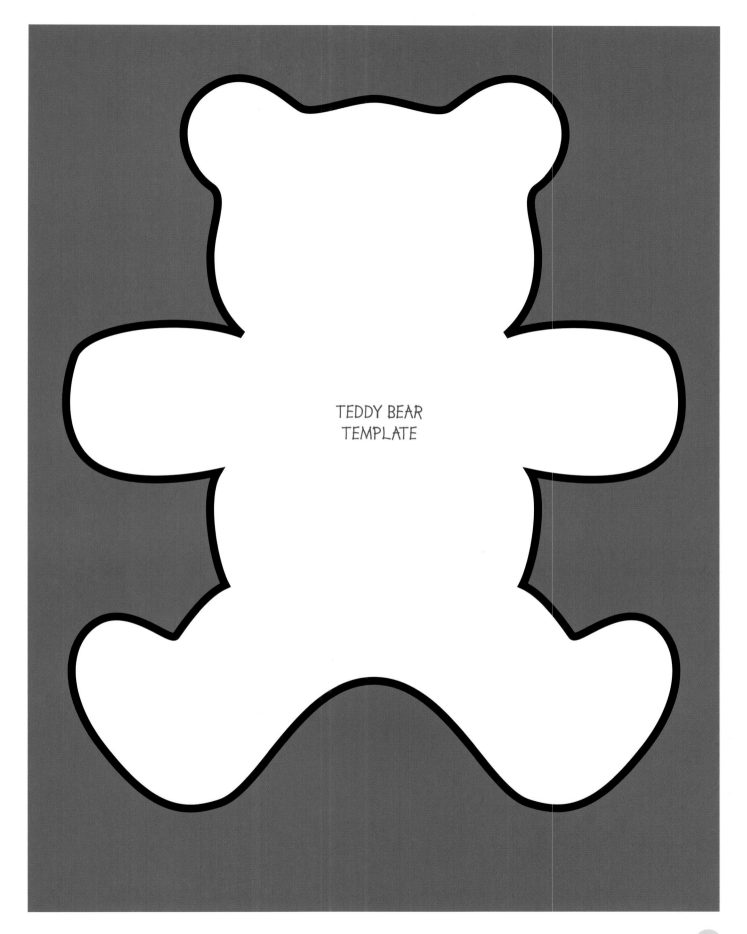

TEDDY BEAR
TEMPLATE

Bunches Of Bears

A group of kids can make lots of bears to share with children near and far. Ask adults to help you find a local organization or shelter where the bears would be welcome, or send the bears away to children in need (such as victims of a flood or other natural disaster) who could use a cuddly animal to call their own. These smaller-sized bears are perfect for kids to keep and take with them.

TRY THIS!

Make Stuffed Animal Toys

After making some bears, you might want to try making other stuffed animal toys. Draw patterns first, as you did with the bear. To make bendable arms and legs, sew together the arms and legs separately and then sew them onto the stuffed animal's body.

TAKE A STITCH

Never sewn before? No problem. Here's a quick look at simple stitches that will do the job.

Running stitch: This stitch is great for making seams. Knot the thread and bring the needle up through the fabric. Work the tip of the needle in and out to create a couple of stitches and then pull the thread through. Continue this way until you finish the seam.

Whipstitch: The whipstitch is used to join two finished edges. Bring the needle from the wrong side of the fabric to the right (finished) side to hide the knot in your thread. Then wrap the thread across the two fabric pieces. Continue whipstitching over the seam until it's closed.

• GLOBAL • CARING •

It's easy to find opportunities to help those in need. You can learn about people in need everywhere in the world in the daily newspaper or on the televised evening news. Sometimes people need help on a daily basis in your own community and must depend on helping hands to survive. Other times, such as when a natural disaster occurs or when there is a world crisis such as a war, people find themselves suddenly in need of help.

Sadly, when disasters strike, people (and animals) may be left without homes, water, or shelter. Many natural disasters (such as floods, mudslides, tornadoes, hurricanes, wildfires, and earthquakes) catch people by surprise. And the same is true for war-torn regions of the world. Often these people do not have time to move their belongings and have to leave everything they own behind. Families, including kids like you, must make do without the usual things we all take for granted — our homes, clothes, toys, and favorite possessions. Giving people an extra boost to help them get started again and letting them know that people *do* care about what is happening to them are both so important. Knowing that others in the world are aware of their plight and are trying to help is comforting to those caught in desperate situations.

Helping others in big and small ways in your town and throughout the world is a great way to show you care. Your efforts to help those in need — both close to your home and even on other continents — will make a real difference for the recipients of your kindness.

There are lots of ways to help right at home, and lots of aid groups you can work with or donate money to for helping on a global scale (see page 123 for a listing of aid organizations), but the basic impulse is similar in all the efforts: Your helping out comes from your willingness to put other people's needs before your own. And that is most admirable — good for you! Start with a scavenger hunt to help gather household necessities or organize a hike for hunger, and then take it from there (check out "Kids Join Together," page 109, too). The more you do, the more the people whose lives you have touched will appreciate your efforts.

Scavenger Hunt to Help

A scavenger hunt is a great way to quickly collect useful items to donate as well as to involve the whole community – plus, it's lots of fun to do! Your group can give the collected items to helping organizations that will appreciate the many donations, such as a relief organization to help victims of natural disasters. When Hurricane Katrina hit Louisiana and Mississippi, people collected blankets and clothes, baby supplies like diapers and formula, emergency medical supplies, and lots of water. Individual groups and towns worked together to send truck caravans loaded with these supplies to the areas in greatest need.

This is an ideal activity for a school, the youth group of a church, mosque, or synagogue, or for Scouts or other service groups.

1 ***Plan a date, time, and place for the hunt.*** Consult with the organization you are helping (such as the local civic, religious, or international aid group) as to the types of items that are most needed and most useful.

2 ***Spread the word.*** Make posters (page 118) to advertise your hunt and the types of items you are looking for (see box on facing page) throughout the community, so that folks will be able to organize their donations ahead of time.

3 **Divide up into teams of players,** with an adult driver or helper for each team, or if you have just a few in your group, go on the hunt together.

4 **Players go door to door,** always working with an adult, to collect the donated items from around the neighborhood or town.

5 **Meet back together at a designated place**. Count up the items to see which team found the most. Award a prize if you like, then arrange to deliver all of the donated items to the helping organization. Aren't you impressed with all the donations? Nice work!

Possible items to hunt for:

- Canned food (vegetables, tuna, beans, etc.) • Boxes of unopened cereal, noodles, hot chocolate, granola bars, and other packaged foods • Mittens, clean and lightly used kids' winter coats, boots • Kitchen or bathroom products (paper towels, toilet paper) • Laundry detergent or cleaning supplies • Baby diapers and baby supplies
- New, wrapped bars of soap, toothbrushes, toothpaste • School supplies
- Good-as-new toys • Good-as-new children's books, videos/DVDs, and CDs

MAKE IT PERSONAL

Imagine what it would feel like to lose your most precious things. Give the gift of a favorite item (like a book or stuffed animal, a model car, or a game) and wrap it with a personal note to the child who will receive it. Knowing that your gift was something very special to you will have so much meaning to the recipient!

ACTS OF CARING

Food drives, meals, and more

Start a monthly food drive in your neighborhood, school, religious center, or other organization to help feed those in need in your community. Plan dates and places to collect, store, and deliver the food. Make posters (page 118) advertising the dates of the food collections, and ask adults to help transport the food to the accepting organization's collecting place. Working together with other kids, you can make a big difference in helping a local food bank fill its empty shelves.

Besides collecting food, you can help the hungry by volunteering at a food bank or at a soup kitchen, or a local organization such as United Way. A group of kids can be a big help sorting and packing food, and volunteering to help prepare and serve free meals at a soup kitchen or shelter is a wonderful way to connect face-to-face with those in need in your community. You may be surprised to realize that needy people and families are people a lot like you who just happen to be experiencing difficult times.

You can also help others far away from where you live by raising money to support groups that help hungry people all over the world (see page 123 for some ideas).

Take a Hike for Hunger

Here's a way to have fun with your friends and family, get some good exercise, and raise money for good causes: Take a hike! You don't need to be near mountains or even out in the country; your hike can be around the city, park, school, or neighborhood. What matters is that you are taking the time to do something that will help others! Donate the money you raise to a group such as CARE or the Global Hunger Project (see list on page 123).

What you need

- Adult helpers
- Maps of your hiking route
- Envelopes

1 Ask adults to help you find a safe place to walk. Walking trails and parks are often good places to hold this event.

2 Ask people of all ages to sign up for the walk. Provide maps and envelopes for donation collections.

3 Set a starting time and place. The more people who hike together, the more attention you will attract for your cause.

4 The walkers ask people they know to sponsor them on the walk ahead of time. Be sure everyone knows how the money is going to be used and what organization the walk is going to help.

5 Collect the money on the day of the event. Then be sure to let everyone know how much money was collected and donated. Take a picture of the top money-raiser to send into the local paper!

MORE FUN! Make "Hike for Hunger" T-shirts

Attract attention to your cause by making T-shirts for each hiker. Paint on logos or pictures to illustrate your event. Use fabric markers to add words or sayings that tell what you hope to accomplish with the money raised, such as "End hunger now!" (For more on decorating T-shirts for a cause, see page 106.)

END HUNGER NOW!

HELP ME HELP THEM Feed the hungry

KIDS CARE ABOUT PETS

Pet animals need love and attention, just as people do! Many pets stay indoors for much of the day while their owners are at school and work. They can become bored easily and gain unneeded weight. Other pets don't get the stimulation and exercise they need because their owners aren't physically able to play with them enough. And cats and dogs at shelters, especially, need a lot of attention to keep them happy, healthy, and socialized.

You can help immediately by playing with pets you know (such as your pets or a neighbor's pets) and by spending time with pets in shelters. To make it more fun, create homemade toys to use as you play with your animal friends! (Remember: never approach a pet you don't know without first asking the owner.)

Another way you can lend a helping hand to keep pets safe and healthy is to make a personalized collar for your pet so that you can be notified easily if your pet gets lost. And you can educate potential pet owners about just what it means to take care of a pet, too. You might even want to join with some friends to raise money and collect supplies for an animal-care group. Organize a dog wash, shoot some pet-and-owners photos, start up a pet play service, and more! It's amazing what a group of kids like you can do when you decide to take action.

No matter which project you choose, you'll feel good about helping to make a furry friend's life a lot better. And just think how grateful your animal pals will be!

• M A K E • C A T • T O Y S •

Playing is a great way for a cat to exercise and stay healthy, just as active play is good for kids like you! You can help cats get exercise by making toys for them to play with and then using the toys in cat playtime. You can even play with cats at shelters, or spend some time with a neighbor's cat that is left alone all day. Check out the ideas on pages 40 and 41 for more ways you can make a difference in the life of a feline friend.

Jingle Chaser

Cats are curious and like to play with toys that move and make a bit of noise. They also love the feel of yarn. Put these cat fancies together to create this enticing cat toy.

What you need

- Small bell
- Empty film canister with lid or section of cardboard tube
- Glue
- Yarn, 3 different colors, 1 yard (m) each
- 2 pom-poms, 1" (2.5 cm) diameter
- Rubber band

1 Put the bell inside the film canister or tube. If using the canister, snap on the lid.

2 Coat the outside of the canister or tube with glue. Wrap one half in one yarn color and the other half in the second color as shown. Add more glue as needed to keep the yarn in place.

3 Cut eight pieces, each 4" (10 cm) long, of the third yarn color. Glue the centers of four pieces in a criss-cross pattern on each pom-pom.

4 Glue a pom-pom, yarn side down, on each end of the canister or tube, and hold in place with a rubber band until the glue dries. Then remove the rubber band and introduce the toy to a cat you know!

CATNAP!

Even if you don't own a cat, you probably know that a "catnap" is a very short, light nap. Cats are experts at relaxing whenever and wherever they can, and some cats seem to nap all the time! Cats love to find comfortable corners, sunny nooks, and soft cushions (or the pile of clean laundry!) where they can curl up and sleep. You can help your cat take a catnap when it needs one with a PERSONALIZED PILLOW (see page 42), but help your feline friend get the exercise it needs, too. Maybe you know a cat that likes to play — only when people want to sleep! Playing with cats during the day helps a cat stay healthy (and helps everyone else in the family sleep better at night).

Create a Home Cat-Care Service!

Many people are busy every day at offices or other places of work. They love their cats, but the cats spend a lot of time at home alone. That's where you come in! Offer to visit their cats after school. Check to see if the cats have enough food and water, and then play with them, using the toys you've made, being sure that the cat gets exercise and gets petted a lot as well. (If the family is going away, ask if you can care for the cat then, too.) For more ideas on creating a pet play service, see page 52.

Keisha's
MOBILE CAT CARE
• COMBING
• FEEDING
• FUN

Cloth Mouse

Cats love to bat around this soft little mouse. For even more feline appeal, add a scoop of catnip (see CATS LOVE CATNIP!, page 38) with the stuffing!

What you need

- Pencil
- Shirt cardboard or heavy paper, cut to 2" x 4" (5 x 10 cm), for the pattern
- Scissors
- Fuzzy fabric, 4" x 4" (10 x 10 cm)
- Fabric marker or pen
- Needle and thread
- Cotton balls
- Catnip, dried (optional)
- Felt scraps
- Yarn, 6" (15 cm)

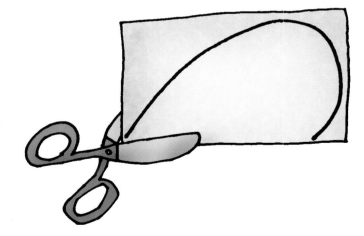

1 Draw half a heart shape on the cardboard so it fills the entire piece as shown. Cut out and label your mouse pattern.

2 Fold the fabric in half, with the fuzzy side facing in. Place the fabric so the folded side is facing you.

3 Place the pattern on the fabric with the flat side along the fold as shown. Trace around the pattern with a fabric marker or pen. With the fabric still folded, cut around the traced shape.

FOLD OF FABRIC

TRACE HERE

4 Thread your needle and knot the end of the thread. Sew the shape together, starting at the pointed end. Stop about an inch (2.5 cm) before the fold, knotting and snipping the thread. Turn the fabric inside out, so the fluffiest side is out and the seam is inside. (You may have to use a pencil to poke the "nose" out.)

DONT KNOW HOW TO SEW? SEE PAGE 24 FOR QUICK-AND-EASY STITCHES.

KNOT THREAD AND START SEWING HERE

FOLD OF FABRIC

KNOT AND SNIP HERE, LEAVING A 1" (2.5 cm) OPENING

5 Stretch out the cotton balls to make them fluffier. Poke the cotton balls inside the mouse's body. Add catnip if you choose. When the body is full, sew it completely closed.

6 Cut out and sew on felt ears and a yarn tail. Draw on eyes and a nose with the fabric marker or pen.

Make "Welcome Toys" for Cats at Shelters

Make enough toys so that you and your friends can deliver them to cats brought to an animal shelter. Call up the shelter ahead of time to schedule your visit (after checking with an adult first, of course). When you bring the toys, play with the cats and pet them so they experience human kindness and playtime. You and your friends might even want to make your visits a weekly event!

CATS LOve CATNIP!

Catnip is a plant related to mint. It has an oil in its hairy, heart-shaped, grayish green leaves that makes many cats go, well, almost wild with joy! You might see them rubbing and rolling on a catnip toy. Sometimes the cats become really silly and more and more playful. Of course, catnip isn't for every cat. Some cats don't respond at all! Other cats might get a little too carried away. If this is the case, ask your vet about how often your cat should play with a catnip-filled toy.

TRY THIS!
Grow Your Own Catnip

If a cat you know likes catnip, you might like to grow your own. Catnip is a perennial plant, so it will grow year after year without having to be replanted. Look for seeds in the herb section of seed racks and follow directions on the package. You can easily grow it in most gardens or in a large container. Harvest the stems full of leaves in late summer, just before the plant flowers. Strip the leaves from the stems and lay them out to dry, out of direct sunlight or in an oven at 150°F (65°C). After the leaves turn crunchy, they can be crumbled and added to cat toys for extra pizzazz.

Yessss!

Cat Tickler

Cats like to try and catch things sweeping through the air, especially anything with feathers!

what you need

- Craft feathers, 2 or 3
- Glue
- Foam packing peanut
- Yarn, 30" (75 cm)
- Toothpick

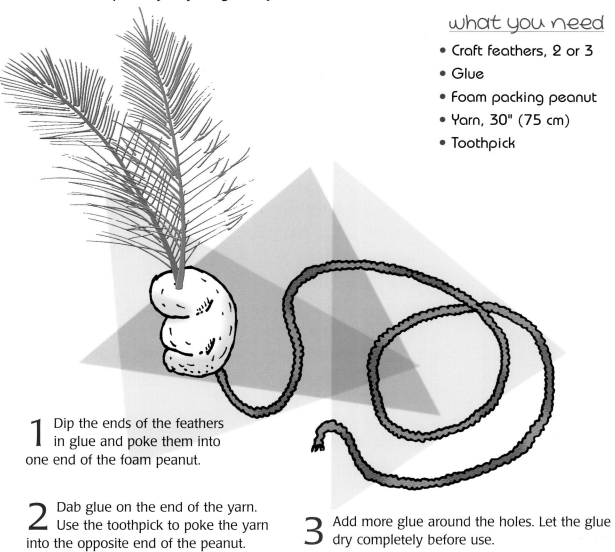

1 Dip the ends of the feathers in glue and poke them into one end of the foam peanut.

2 Dab glue on the end of the yarn. Use the toothpick to poke the yarn into the opposite end of the peanut.

3 Add more glue around the holes. Let the glue dry completely before use.

MORE FUN! Quick-as-a-wink cat toys

Need a cat toy in a hurry? Use a small ball of yarn or string as an instant toy, or tie a scrap of cloth onto one end of a piece of string so you can drag it across the floor or wave it in the air. Once the cat sees the motion, it will want to join in on the fun!

CAT GAMES

Here are some simple ways you can share your cat-toy creations with a feline friend that's in your care. Thanks to you, the cat will get plenty of exercise while it's having fun playing.

Go Fetch

Use the JINGLE CHASER, the CLOTH MOUSE, or a ball of yarn to play a game of fetch. Some cats will learn to retrieve a toy that is thrown for them. Others will not! In either case, cats enjoy a game of chase. Toss the yarn ball in places that give the cat a chance to climb, jump, and run.

Sneaky Peek

Cats like to wait and watch before suddenly pouncing on a toy. If the cat has claws, tie a string to a small ball of yarn or to the CLOTH MOUSE or JINGLE CHASER. Play Sneaky Peek by placing the toy in front of the cat. Ever so slowly, begin to move the toy by pulling on the string. This will get the cat's interest. Hide the toy or yarn ball under a sheet of paper, around a corner, or partway under a piece of cloth. Hold the toy or yarn ball still again. Now begin to move it slowly. Soon the cat will try to catch it. Move the toy faster by pulling and jerking the string. Let the cat catch the toy now and again so that it doesn't get frustrated.

Catnap Tickle

Wake a sleeping cat gently with the CAT TICKLER. A soft feather lightly brushed against a cat's sensitive ears, paws, or nose is sure to get its attention. Cats often like to roll on their backs and bat at the cat tickler if you circle it in the air above them. To get even more cat action, swing it as if it were flying through the air.

ACTS OF CARING

Raise money for cat clinics!

You can help cats in two ways with this kids' cat-care idea. First, you can offer to care for friends' and neighbors' cats (see page 34). Then, you can donate the money you earn to a special fund at a shelter or clinic for cats so that people can have their cats neutered (to cut down on the numbers of strays and homeless cats that are dropped off at animal shelters) and vaccinated. You'll help keep unwanted cats from being hungry and homeless, and keep the cats you love from getting sick.

How Much Exercise Is Good for Cats?

Cats get tired quickly. Their bodies are built for bursts of speed and exercise between long naps. Play active games for 5 or 10 minutes at a time. Young cats and kittens need more exercise and can play more often than older cats. Panting and rapid heartbeat are signs that a cat is getting tired. You should stop playing with a cat that is showing signs of fatigue, and never force a cat to play. If a cat loses interest in playing, take a break and play again later.

Personalized Pillow

Make a fluffy pillow bed to give your furry cat friend (or a small dog) a soft place to sleep. (Maybe then it will stay out of the laundry basket!) You might also like to make several of these pillow beds for shelter animals. (Call the shelter first to see if it would be able to use them. Be sure to let the shelter know your pillows are washable.) A soft bed can help a shelter animal get a better rest!

what you need

- Paper and pencil or colored markers and scrap paper
- Solid-colored pillowcase
- Nontoxic fabric paints or markers
- Old pillow (one that has flattened out and isn't too firm)

1 Use paper and pencil or markers to sketch out your design first, so that you have an idea of how it will fit on the fabric.

2 Decorate one side of the pillow case with fabric paints or markers (the other side will be against the floor). Let dry.

3 Slip the pillow inside, and set the pillow bed in one of your cat's favorite sleeping spots. Soon your cat will know this is where it belongs!

• MAKE • DOG • TOYS •

Dogs need exercise too — every day! Keep pet dogs (and yourself!) in shape by playing games with homemade toys. Dogs in shelters, pet stores, and recovery centers need toys and playtime, too. Make extra toys for these animals, and while you're visiting, ask if the centers need volunteers to play with and exercise the dogs.

Ball Flinger

This very simple toy is sure to become a dog's favorite. The sock makes the ball easy for the dog to see and catch, and fun for you to throw.

what you need

- Tennis or rubber ball
- Old sock (a long soccer-type athletic sock works best)

1 Place the ball inside the sock right down in the toe area.

2 Tie knots in the sock at the opening and in one or two more places along its length. Now, fling it!

Stuffed Bone

Dogs love to shake and chew a stuffed toy. Keep your own stuffed toys safe and a dog happy by making a special dog-only toy. Expect it to get plenty of use! Bring it out for special games of fetch (see page 46) with your furry pal.

•BONE-MAKING TIP•

To make the bone pattern symmetrical, fold the paper into fourths. Draw a quarter of a bone on the folded paper as shown. The shape will look like a letter *P*. Be sure the shape includes the folded sides of the paper. Cut along your lines, and then open the folds. Presto, a perfect bone!

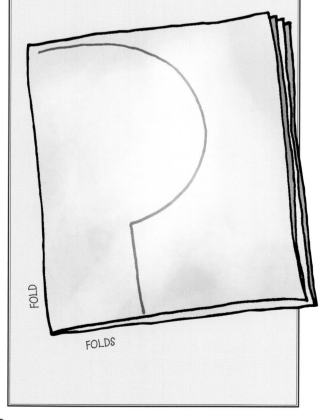

what you need

- Pencil
- Paper, 8½" x 11" (21 x 27.5 cm)
- Scissors
- Durable fabric (canvas, denim, twill), 2 pieces each 9" x 12" (22.5 x 30 cm) *Reuse and save resources by cutting fabric from the legs of an old pair of jeans!*
- Straight pins
- Marker or pen
- Fabric scissors
- Needle and thread
- Sewing machine (optional)
- Soft toy or pillow stuffing (found at fabric and craft stores)
- Nontoxic fabric markers

1 Draw the shape of a bone so it fills the piece of paper to make your patten (see BONE-MAKING TIP, facing page). Cut out the shape and label your pattern.

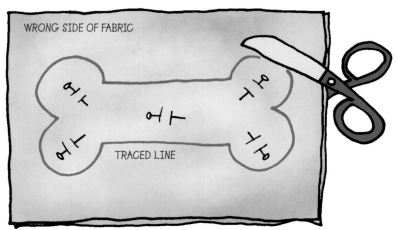

WRONG SIDE OF FABRIC

TRACED LINE

FACE RIGHT SIDES OF FABRIC TOGETHER (INSIDE)

2 Lay the two pieces of fabric together so their right (finished) sides are together, facing in. Pin the pattern on top of the fabric pieces and trace around it with a marker or pen.

3 Use fabric scissors to cut through the fabric pieces. (If it is too difficult to cut through both pieces of fabric at once, cut them out one at a time.)

START HERE   END HERE

4 Thread the needle and knot the end of the thread. With the two fabric shapes still pinned, sew around the edges with a running stitch (see TAKE A STITCH, page 24, for a quick sewing lesson), ¼" (5 mm) in from the outer edge of the fabric, leaving a 2" (5 cm) opening along one of the straight sides as shown. Use small stitches placed close together to make your sewing strong. Or, ask an adult to help you use a sewing machine. Knot and snip the thread.

SKIPPY

5 Remove all pins. Turn the bone right side out.

6 Fill the bone with stuffing, using a pencil to poke stuffing into the ends of the bone. Sew the opening closed with a needle and thread.

7 Add decorations and words with fabric markers to personalize your dog's new toy.

MORE FUN! Quick-as-a-wink dog toy

An old tennis ball is always a hit with the canine crowd.

PLAY, DOG, PLAY!

Almost all dogs like a game of fetch, and the BALL FLINGER and STUFFED BONE work great for this game. Add variety by throwing the toy in different directions. Throwing the toy high in the air gives a dog a chance to try and catch it; throwing it far gives lots of running exercise.

You might also like to set up a safe obstacle course for a small dog. The dog could climb over pillows, through an open-ended box tunnel, or around soft obstacles to get to the toy.

Be sure to keep the play safe for the dog. Never throw a toy in the direction of a street, sharp object, or up on something the animal could fall from. Dogs don't get tired as quickly as cats do (see page 41), but you still need to watch for signs of fatigue. Let the dog rest when its panting gets rapid or after playing hard for 15 minutes. Offer the dog plenty of water after exercising.

START

Make Homemade Dog Biscuits!

It's tempting to give dogs scraps, but as you probably know, "people food" isn't a healthy habit for pets. (People food is OK for humans, but it's not a balanced food for dogs.) Instead, try this recipe for healthy, teeth-cleaning, yummy dog biscuits so you'll be ready the next time a dog you love needs a treat!

    While you're cooking up a batch of homemade treats, make extra to share with dogs in shelters, guide-dog or police-dog training schools, and anywhere else dogs live or work in your community. Just be sure to check with the dog's owner that a treat is OK for the pet to have; working dogs shouldn't be distracted from their jobs (you can just donate a bag of the treats to the owner or organization instead). Treats may also come in handy when you're dog-sitting (see *Start a Pet Play Service!*, page 52), but, again, check before feeding someone else's pet.

what you need

- ⅓ cup (5⅓ tablespoons/75 ml) margarine, softened
- Large mixing bowl
- 1 cup (250 ml) uncooked oatmeal
- 3½ cups (875 ml) whole-wheat flour, plus extra for rolling
- Fork
- Large spoon
- 1 egg
- ½ cup (125 ml) milk
- 1 cup (250 ml) chicken broth
- 1 cup (250 ml) shredded cheddar cheese
- Rolling pin and cloth, cookie cutters, baking sheet, and rack
- Spatula

Makes about 18 biscuits.

1 Soften the margarine in the bowl. Mix in the oatmeal and 1 cup (250 ml) of the flour with a fork until the mixture is crumbly. Stir in the egg, milk, and chicken broth. Then add another cup (250 ml) of flour. Stir in the cheese, and add the remaining flour a little at a time until dough is well mixed.

2 Sprinkle the cloth and rolling pin with flour. Roll out dough ½" (1 cm) thick and cut into shapes with cookie cutters.

3 Place shapes on a greased baking sheet. Bake at 325°F (160°C) for 25 to 30 minutes. Remove from sheet with a spatula and let cool completely on the rack. Store biscuits in a paper bag in the refrigerator to keep them fresh and crunchy.

•FEEDING TIPS•

Feed large dogs an entire biscuit or crumble biscuits into small bits to feed to smaller dogs or cats. As with any pet treat, be careful not to give too many treats (a few a day will be plenty), and use caution feeding an animal you don't know well. Be sure to check with the owner before feeding any animal that is not yours.

Raise Money for Pet-Care Centers and Shelters

Gather your friends to make lots of biscuits to sell to raise money for clinics or pet care shelters. Your group might try selling the dog treats at pet-food stores, craft fairs, or your local grocery store. Get permission first, then bake away! Decide on a name for your dog biscuits, and list the ingredients on the bag so pet owners know what they're buying. The dogs will love it, and you'll feel proud about raising money for a good cause! For more on fund-raising basics, see page 120.

Host a Dog Wash

A dog wash is a wet and wild event that is sure to please dog owners! This is definitely a project where a group of kids is needed. Don't forget to wear clothes that can get wet! Money earned from a dog wash might go to help humane societies, shelters, or pet rescue organizations, or to fund other animal-care projects. (For a list of organizations, see page 123.)

what you need

- Hose with an adjustable nozzle
- Dog shampoo (see note on page 52)
- Wading pool (optional)
- Buckets
- Plastic cups or bowls
- Dog brush
- Towels
- Dog treats (see page 47 to make your own!)
- Index cards and a pen, or a computer, to make tickets
- Notebook (optional)

1 Decide where to have the dog wash, and get permission to use this space. Be sure your chosen spot has an outdoor faucet.

2 Plan a day and time for the dog wash. Check the weather forecast, and choose a warm, sunny day. Have an alternate date in mind if the weather isn't good!

3 Gather washing supplies. Practice washing a friendly dog you know. Pay attention to how long it takes and the steps needed. Remember, you'll need extra time for changing the water and preparing for the next dog.

4　Divide up the jobs so that everyone in the group has a job. Two kids can hold and comfort the dog, while other kids have jobs of washing, rinsing, drying, and brushing. Or teams of two to three kids can take turns washing, rinsing, and drying different dogs.

5　Decide how much to charge per dog wash. The cost should be less than someone would pay elsewhere in town, but enough to make money after expenses.

6　On index cards or on the computer, make tickets that include the name of your group, the event, and a blank space to write in a time. Giving appointments helps you manage time and keeps people and dogs from waiting.

7　Sell tickets to neighbors, friends, and relatives. Be sure to explain how the money is going to be used. As you describe your project, ask to see the dog and make sure it is friendly and easy to pet and handle. Tell owners they will need to stay with their dog during the wash in case the dog gets scared or hard to control.

8　Organize a page in a notebook or in the computer to keep track of the dog-washing appointments. Include a phone number in case you need to call and remind an owner about an appointment.

9　Hope for a warm, sunny day on the day of your big event! Then follow the steps on page 51 to wash each dog.

HOW TO WASH A DOG

1. Fill buckets with warm water (be careful it doesn't get too hot).

2. Brush the dog to get out tangles and bits of dirt or leaves.

3. Gently pour cupfuls of water over the dog, starting at the back and moving up. Be sure to reach the legs and belly. Do not pour water on the dog's head.

4. Follow the directions on the bottle of dog shampoo. Use the smallest amount of shampoo suggested. Gently rub the shampoo into the fur, being careful not to get any around the face. Use plain water and a washcloth to clean the face.

5. Rinse off the shampoo with scoops of water or use a gentle spray from a hose. Make sure all the shampoo is rinsed off.

6. Let the dog shake if it wants to and finish drying the fur with a towel.

7. Reward the dog with kind words and a treat!

TRY THIS!

Pool Fun

A wading pool is handy to have for a dog wash. Place it in the sun and fill it with a few inches (cm) of water. Some dogs won't mind jumping into the pool. This wastes less water and makes it easier to scoop water over their fur. Use the bucket method if a dog is afraid to get in the pool.

RIBBIT!

THE SCOOP ON DOG SHAMPOO

Human shampoo is not mild enough for a dog's skin and fur, so it's best to use a pet shampoo or bar for your dog wash. Read the labels carefully before you choose. Find a mild shampoo suitable for all types of dogs. Don't buy flea-killing shampoo, as it can be harmful to your skin and eyes, and not all dogs will need it.

Start a Pet Play Service!

Help busy pet owners give their pets the attention and exercise they need. Offer to help out a family friend who is elderly or a dog owner who needs to work long hours. The pet owners will appreciate the time you spend playing with their pets and providing them with the exercise they need to stay healthy. You can also get a group of friends together to pool your pet-care efforts. Use the money you raise to support a pet clinic or donate it to an animal shelter, an organization such as your local branch of the Humane Society (www.hsus.org), or to another pet-care project, such as CREATIVE COLLARS (see page 56) or pet tags.

Patty's Pet Play Service

In business since last week

what you need

- Paper and pen
- Notebook or computer (for scheduling)
- Pet-care flyer (optional)
- A variety of pet toys (to make your own, see pages 32, 35, and 43!)

1 Make a list of pet owners everyone in the group knows. Decide together on a name for your pet play service.

Safety First!

Never go to the house of someone you don't know. When pet-sitting, be sure you tell your parents or guardians where you are going and give them a copy of your pet play schedule. Play with pets with a partner, if possible. If you feel uncomfortable in a house or with a pet, you can always leave the pet safe inside and go home.

2 Make a chart of times each person is available to play with pets. Find times when members are free to work together. (It's more fun and safer to partner up to play with an animal.) Plan pet playing sessions for 30 minutes.

3 Create a flyer that includes the name of your pet play service, why exercising a pet is important, the times your group members are available, the cost of each session, and a contact phone number. (For pointers on making a flyer, see page 117.)

4 Call and visit the pet owners on your list. Explain the purpose of your group and the reason you are raising money. Hand out flyers to people you know who want to think about it before scheduling. Give flyers to other pet owners you learn about through friends and family.

5 Schedule pet playing sessions on a computer spreadsheet or chart or in a notebook. Include any specific information about each pet owner's needs and details or routines you want to remember about the pet.

Pet Partner Photo

Pets are a part of the family! Pet owners will like to have fun photos taken with their pets to include in family photo albums and scrapbooks, and it's a great way for you and your friends to raise money for pet-care projects.

what you need

- Camera (digital or film)
- Computer (optional)
- Flyer or poster

1 Practice taking photos of people within your group's families. Experiment taking pictures in different locations, from various angles, and in indoor and outdoor lighting. See tips on page 55.

2 Look over the photos and discuss which ones are best and why. You will probably notice that moving closer to the subjects creates a better picture. You will also want to pay attention to lighting and the background.

3 Decide the best place to use as your photo studio. Outdoors is easier because you don't need to use a flash or set up a background.

4 Figure out how much it costs to make one photograph. Add up film and processing or photo paper and printer cartridges and divide it by the number of photos printed. Use this information to decide on a price for your pet photos. Charge enough to cover costs and add extra to make a small profit.

5 Create a flyer or poster (see pages 117 and 118) to explain your service. Feature a sample photo. Also include your group's name, contact phone number, and cost per photo.

6 Hand out the flyers to friends, family, and neighbors. Ask pet supply stores, vet clinics, and pet stores if you can display your posters or leave flyers with them.

7 Schedule photo sessions on days when members are available. If shooting outdoors, make a rain date in case of bad weather.

8 Keep track of the money spent and made. Donate the profits to a pet cause.

•PHOTO TIPS•

• Side lighting works best to help show faces without making eyes squint.

• Avoid poles, cars, and clutter in the background.

• Zoom in as close as possible.

• Try to catch the person with a natural smile or laugh. You can do this by talking to them and then snapping the picture before they get ready to pose.

• If the pet doesn't want to sit still, try some action shots of the owner playing with its animal.

TRY THIS!

Pet Holiday Cards

Your group might also custom-design holiday cards for pet owners. Photos can be printed on special computer cards or glued to folded construction paper. (See page 10 for more card ideas.)

Creative Collars

A lost dog or cat cannot explain where it lives. It is easier to reunite a pet with its owners if it's wearing a collar that tells the pet's name and phone number or address. Some pet owners have tags on their pets that include the contact information, but many others don't get around to that. This project will help you get your pet back in a hurry if it strays away.

what you need

- Solid-colored fabric or nylon pet collar
- Permanent markers or paint pens

1 Purchase a pet collar to fit your pet.

2 Clearly print the pet's name and a phone number or address on the collar with the markers or pens.

3 Add other decorations, but make sure the contact information remains visible.

Help Prevent Lost Pets

Keep the animals you love and know safe by making sure they have the collars, licenses, and tags or IDs required by your town. If your pet's collar is already labeled, alert other pet owners to the importance of tagging their furry friends. Set up a booth (see page 119) at a pet supply store or other store or park where pets are allowed. Supply permanent markers and show your sample collars and pet tags. When people stop by with their pets, encourage them to put contact information on their pet's collar. You could also make posters to remind pet owners about the due dates in your town for purchasing dog or cat licenses. Or provide information to pet owners about keeping their pet contained. Distribute the information as a bookmark or flyer (see page 117) at animal shelters.

If you do see a pet that seems lost, don't try to pick up or follow the animal. (It might be sick or afraid and could bite you, and it's not safe for you to follow a lost pet on your own.) Call the animal shelter to pick up the pet so the owners can find it. (If there are tags on the pet, the shelter workers will be able to match the pet to the owner.) You can also offer to make posters for people you know who have a lost pet. Post them at local grocery stores, banks, coffee shops, gas stations, and the town community center or library.

Pet-Care Primer

Taking care of a pet is a big responsibility. It is important for new or potential pet owners to have lots of information to help them give their pet the care it needs and to understand what owning a pet really means in terms of time, cost, and care. You and your friends can help by finding out what pets' needs are and making a flyer or brochure to educate other kids. Share important facts and helpful tips about feeding, immunizations, exercising, and keeping a pet-friendly house. And if you don't yet own a pet, this is a good way to figure out if you are ready for one. Pets provide love and companionship to humans, but they must depend on their owners for everything: food, water, exercise, and socialization. Making a pet-care primer is a great way for you and your friends to help make sure your furry friends are loved and cared for properly!

what you need

- Notebook and pencil
- Veterinarian(s)
- Library
- Computer and printer
- Poster board
- Colored paper and markers
- Camera (film or digital)
- Glue

1 Find out what information is most important about caring for a dog or cat. Ask to set up a 10-minute interview with one or more veterinarians. Explain how you are helping give new pet owners pointers about pet care. Ask them to share some of the most important things pet owners should know. Be careful to write down what they say accurately and ask them to repeat or explain anything you are unclear about.

2 Look at pet books in the library. Read and take notes about the most important things people need to know about caring for pets. Choose a few of the top facts or tips.

3 Decide the best way to write the information so people will notice it and read it. Design a flyer, brochure, booklet, bookmark, or poster (see pages 116 to 118 for details). Or make up a pet-care quiz for potential pet owners (see page 60 for ideas). Ask someone to read over your work to make sure it is correct and makes sense. Add pictures, photographs, and decorations to the final version.

4 Make copies and distribute to adoption shelters, veterinarians, and pet stores.

❓ Dog-Care Quiz

Are you ready for a pet? Take this quiz and see how you do!

Have you ever had to care for something every day, whether you wanted to or not?

Who would walk your dog during the day while you are in school? In the morning before school?

Do you have other pets that might not get along with the dog?

Where would your dog stay if you went away?

Do you know how much it costs to feed a dog? Do you have a job or chores you get paid for to help with expenses?

Is there a park nearby that allows dogs to run loose for exercise? If not, how would your dog get enough exercise?

Who would walk the dog in rain, snow, and other bad weather?

Who would get up early on Saturday morning to walk the dog or leave a ballgame early to walk the dog?

Do you live in a big house or a small apartment? Is there room for a dog?

If your dog rolls in something smelly, where will you wash it?

What covers a tree?

Bark!

How does sandpaper feel?

Ruff!

With a smart dog like you, do I really need school?

Yip.

KIDS CARE ABOUT WILDLIFE

The pets you share your home with depend on you for a place to sleep, food to eat, and a way to play and exercise. But there are other animals who also call where you live "home": the wildlife all around you. Each animal has its own *habitat,* or home where it has a place to sleep, food to eat, water to drink, and somewhere safe to move around. Wild animals have trouble finding homes and food when forests are cut down and wetlands drained to make way for houses and farms, so any habitat help we can give helps our animal friends.

Learn about local animals by becoming a wildlife watcher, by taking a nature count, and by going on a scavenger hunt for animal clues. Make feeders and houses for your feathered friends, and plant a patch of sunflowers to feed birds, insects, and other animals. You can even grow special gardens for butterflies and bees! Use your talents to help protect and care for parks and other natural areas in your town where wildlife can flourish.

You can help endangered animals who live all around the world, too. Teach others about animals that are in danger. Brainstorm ways to raise money for endangered-animal organizations, and then take action. You'll be amazed at how much you can do to help!

No matter what project you choose, you are sure to feel good knowing you are helping other animals on the planet. (Remember, we are animals, too!)

Become a Wildlife Watcher!

Have you ever seen a squirrel take a death-defying leap from tree to tree, watched a bird feed its young, followed a grasshopper, or watched a butterfly sipping nectar? All around us, wildlife are doing amazing things. When we take the time to observe them, we begin to understand animal habits and needs, making it easier to know how to help. You and your friends can even form a wildlife watchers club! (See page 109 for more group ideas.) Check the kit on the facing page for a list of handy supplies.

Choose some favorite wildlife-watching sites. These places might include gardens or flower beds (see pages 71 and 76 for planting your own!); a favorite tree, bush, or cactus; along a fencerow or the side of a house or barn; a local park or natural area; next to a pond or creek — even a back porch or a balcony on an apartment building can be a good spot to see wildlife.

Listen carefully. Sit quietly and listen to the sounds around you. Do you hear birds singing or insects buzzing? Leaves rustling? The *tap, tap, tap* of a woodpecker? The sound of a garbage can being overturned at night?

Look closely. Look up to the tops of trees and buildings. Can you spot branches moving or movement on utility lines? Look at the ground for droppings or feathers. Do you spy crawling insects? Keep still and see if animals get used to you and return to their normal activities.

Dig a little deeper. Ask permission to dig in the garden (if you have one) or in a patch of dirt. What critters can you find crawling in the soil?

Record what you notice. Record the time and place of your wildlife watch in a notebook. Write down what wildlife you can hear or see. Draw sketches of anything that interests you. Take photos that can later be added to the pages of your notebook.

Compare the different animals you observe from one place to another. Keep records in your notebook and see what changes through the seasons.

WILDLIFE WATCHER'S KIT

Your senses — especially listening, seeing, and smelling — are your most important tools for wildlife sleuthing. Here are a few other items that can make wildlife watching easier.

WOW!

- Hand lens or magnifying glass
- Binoculars
- Sketchbook or notebook
- Pencil or pen for writing observations
- Colored pencils for drawing
- Trowel or large spoon for digging
- Flashlight, for nighttime viewing
- Field guides to birds and other wildlife, for identification (optional)
- Bug net (optional)
- Camera, to record your wildlife sightings!

Safety First!

Wild Animal Ahead: Do Not Handle!

No matter how cute a wild animal is, remember that it is *wild*. Never approach or handle a wild animal. Some wild animals may carry rabies or other diseases, and any wild animal will be scared of you and may try to bite. Always watch wildlife from a safe distance. This is best for the animal, too!

Unlike your pets, wild animals are accustomed to living on their own. They need special food and care that only Mother Nature can provide. Most wild critters will die if they are captured and taken from their habitat. So never bring a wild animal home, no matter how tame it appears! You want to leave your animal friends right where they belong, out in the wild.

Join a Nature Count

You and your friends can join one of the many nature counts to help scientists learn more about animal populations in your area. Counts are compared from year to year to discover how populations change. The thing is, all these counts depend on people just like you to carry them out. By helping out, you are contributing to some very important research! The organizations listed below will help you get started. Go to the web sites to discover how to make an official count of birds, butterflies, or frogs. Then follow the directions to organize your own count. And thanks for caring enough to count!

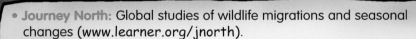

- **Journey North:** Global studies of wildlife migrations and seasonal changes (www.learner.org/jnorth).

- **National Audubon Society Christmas Bird Count:** A one-day winter tally taken throughout the U.S. and Canada and parts of Central and South America every year (www.audubon.org/bird/cbc/).

- **The Great Backyard Bird Count:** A four-day count of bird populations across North, Central, and South America in mid-February that helps researchers determine how winter weather influences bird populations (www.birdsource.org/gbbc).

- **Project FeederWatch:** A winter-long count of birds that visit feeders (like yours!) throughout North America (www.birds.cornell.edu/pfw).

- **Monarch Watch:** Counts that help with the conservation, research, and education about monarch butterflies (www.monarchwatch.org).

- **Frogwatch USA:** Long-term monitoring of frog and toad populations (www.nwf.org/frogwatchUSA/).

Spread the Word on Wildlife Awareness

Share the results of your nature counts and animal scavenger hunt (see page 66) with younger kids and adults in your community to raise awareness of the need for animal habitats. Make posters (see page 118) that explain your wildlife watcher findings. Ask others if they'd like to help start a wildlife habitat at your school, community center, church, or synagogue. Work with a local park to keep a section of the park as a natural habitat. You could also sow sunflowers and milkweed (see pages 71 and 79) and plant a butterfly garden (see page 76). All over the country, kids like you are teaming up to transform school yards and community places into wildlife-friendly green spots.

MORE FUN! Make a blind

Tie branches onto a lawn chair to help you blend in while you sit in comfort. This is not necessary for wildlife watching, but it sure is a lot of fun!

Animal-Clue Scavenger Hunt

This is a great group game to play at a park, nature center, or even in a city neighborhood, and it helps you and your friends become more aware of the wildlife living in your community. All you need is some paper and pencils, and a good spot to scavenge for animal clues! For even more fun, work in teams to find the clues.

The setup

1 Make a list of animals and animal signs that it is possible to locate in the area you choose. Here are some suggestions to include on the list:

- Bird nest
- Ant carrying something
- Woodpecker hole
- Spider web
- Worm casting
- Leaf chewed by an insect
- Feather
- Ground burrow
- Bark beetle tracks
- Bird calling
- Squirrel's nest

2 Copy the list for each team or player. Set up the boundaries of the hunt (within a backyard, or an area of a park, or other easy boundary). Agree on a time to meet back together.

To play

Players check off any clues they find. The team that finds the most clues wins!

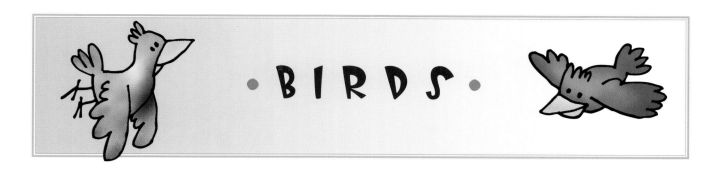

· B I R D S ·

Window Art (It's for the Birds!)

Have you ever heard a "bump" and then found a bird beneath your window? Millions of birds fly into windows each year. Many are killed, while others are just stunned and are able to fly away after recovering.

Birds fly into windows because they see the reflection of the landscape in the glass. You can help birds notice the glass by making removable stick-on decorations for your windows. Make extra window art to help friends and relatives save the birds at their homes and workplaces.

what you need

- Pencil
- Paper
- Colored plastic sheets (report covers or laminating plastic works well)
- Permanent markers
- Scissors
- Sponge
- Towel
- Tape (optional)

1 Draw window-art pictures on paper. Make flowers, birds, butterflies, or backyard animals, or choose your own design idea. Keep the shapes big enough to be seen from a distance.

2 Place the plastic over your drawings. Use markers to copy the designs on the plastic. Add more colors and details. Let the ink dry.

3 Carefuly cut around your window art.

4 Moisten the backs of the shapes with a damp sponge, then stick the shapes on the window. Use a towel to press the shapes tight to the glass. Window art sticks from the bond of water to glass. If the art falls off, simply remoisten the plastic and press it back on the window or attach with tape.

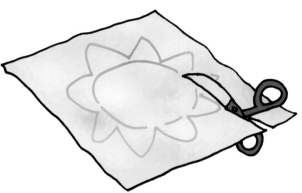

Has anyone seen my *Greatest Hits of the Purple Surfing Cowboys* cd?

TRY THIS!

Create CD Shiners

Another way to keep birds from flying into windows is to hang unwanted CDs in front of the glass. They work especially well if they are hung so that they can move freely in the wind. The shiny surface will distract birds and keep them away.

Bird-Shapes Window Art

Check in bird books and field guides for the names and pictures of common birds in your area. Trace the images onto clear plastic sheets and color the birds according to the guide information. Write the name of the birds at the bottom of the window art. Give your bird-shapes window art as gifts or sell them at a "HELP THE ANIMALS" FAIR (see page 85) or other local fund-raiser. You'll be helping the birds and educating people about the birds common to their area at the same time!

Make a Milk-Jug Bird Feeder

Bird feeders are an easy and fun way to get a closer look at our feathered friends, and the birds will appreciate the snack, especially during the winter months when Mother Nature's fare can be harder to find. This simple feeder not only helps the birds, but also helps the environment by reusing a milk jug.

what you need

- Plastic gallon milk jug
- Permanent marker
- Ruler
- Scissors
- Wooden dowels, 2,
  ³⁄₈" (8.5 mm) in diameter
  and 10" (25 cm) long
- Wire
- Birdseed

1 Wash out the milk jug. Mark a 4" (10 cm) square 2" (5 cm) up from the bottom on each of the two flat sides as shown. Cut along the sides and bottom lines of the squares, with adult help if needed. Bend up the flaps to make a roof over each opening.

2 Poke a hole below each opening and through the opposite sides of the jug. Stick the two dowels through the holes, forming an X.

3 Bend wire around the top of the jug for a hanger and twist to fasten.

4 Hang the bird feeder from a tree or pole, filled with an inch (2.5 cm) of birdseed.

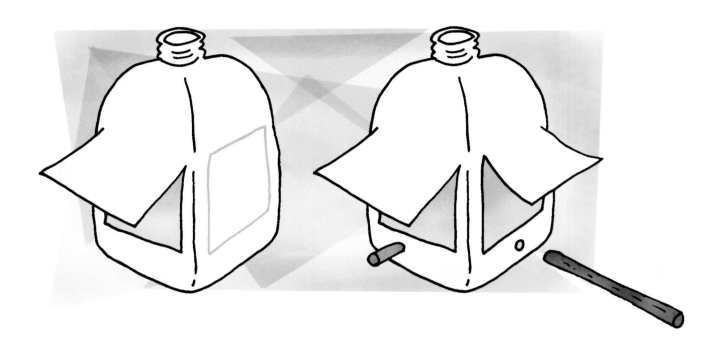

ACTS OF CARING

No-Fuss Furnishings

Help birds "feather their nests" by supplying an assortment of the nest-building materials listed below. Leave them where they can be easily spotted, such as in a basket on the lawn. Then, watch for familiar bits of material poking out of birdhouses and nests!

- fabric scraps, cut into small strips   • string and yarn in short pieces
- dryer lint   • cotton balls   • cut grass

Serve Up Some Sunflowers

Sunflower seeds are a nutritious food for many kinds of birds and squirrels, and they're fun and easy to grow. Simply find a patch of soil that gets plenty of sunshine (against a house, along a sidewalk, or by a fence), or plant the seeds in a large pot. There are many varieties of sunflowers — some are small and some grow taller than you are! Look at seed packages to find the variety that produces lots of plump seeds and grows well where you live. Follow the directions on the package for planting and care. You'll be rewarded with big, bright blooms in late summer!

You can let the wildlife eat the seeds right from the plant, or you can dry and store the seeds for feeders. Sunflower heads are actually many flowers all in one. Every seed forms from its own tiny flower on the head that is surrounded by colorful yellow petals. Harvest the seeds in late summer, after the petals begin to fall off. Cut stalks about a foot (30 cm) below the flower head. Hang it upside down in a dry place until seeds become dry and hard. Pluck the seeds from the head and store them in bags. Don't forget to save some of the seeds to plant next year's flowers!

Birds that like sunflower seeds include cardinals, jays, nuthatches, titmice, finches, grosbeaks, blackbirds, sparrows, woodpeckers, and indigo buntings. Some types of butterflies like sunflowers too! (See CREATE A BUTTERFLY RETREAT, page 76.)

Recycled Birdhouse

Birds need food and shelter for raising their young. Here's a simple single-season birdhouse you can make from recycled materials. Give some birds in your area a summer retreat!

what you need

- Cardboard milk or juice carton, half-gallon size
- Disposable container (for mixing paint)
- Dish soap
- Measuring cup
- Exterior acrylic paint and paintbrush
- Ruler
- Scissors
- Piece of wire mesh or window screening, 3½" x 7½" (9 x 19 cm)
- Marker
- Stapler
- Plastic lid, cut into a 4" (10 cm) square
- Hot-glue gun and glue sticks
- Stiff wire

1 Wash and rinse the carton. Mix a squirt of dish soap with ½ cup (125 ml) of paint. Paint the outside of the carton. Let dry. Apply a second coat and let dry.

2 Choose a front for the birdhouse from one of the sides with a sloping top. Measure and cut a hole 1½" (3.5 cm) in diameter — or choose the hole size best for the bird you want to attract (see page 74) — 2" (5 cm) down from the top edge.

3 Place the screening or wire mesh inside the carton against the front panel. Trace around the outside hole with a marker; remove the mesh and cut out the traced hole. Reinsert the mesh and staple it in place at the top.

5 Ask an adult to help you poke the following holes in the carton:

- Five or six holes in the bottom to allow rainwater to drain from the house.
- Holes at the top and bottom back corners of each side for hanging.
- Several small holes near the top to allow fresh air into the house.

4 Staple the top of carton closed. Add hot glue along top edge to seal it. Fasten the plastic lid to the front sloping side of the carton with hot glue. (This will help keep rain away from the entrance.)

6 To hang the house, poke a piece of wire in one side and out the other at the top and twist together to form a loop. Repeat with a second piece of wire at the bottom. Fasten the wires to a pole, tree, or mounting board.

MORE FUN! Add some twigs!

Add to the natural look of the birdhouse by hot-gluing thin twigs on the sides and roof.

Make a Simple Gourd Birdhouse!

You can grow large gourds to turn into cozy homes for birds. A gourd birdhouse sways in the breeze, so it is less likely to be bothered by predators, and the birdhouse will last for years. Look for birdhouse gourds at farm-stands in the fall, or grow your own. Ask an adult to help you drill the entrance hole. Check with some birding experts or online at the National Audubon Society site, www.audubon.org, about the correct hole size for the bird you want to attract, as different birds like different opening sizes on their houses. A purple martin needs a 2½" (6 cm) hole, while a little house wren requires only a 1" (2.5 cm) hole! Drill some drainage holes and holes for hanging as shown, and varnish or paint the outside of the house (white is the recommended color for attracting purple martins; use brown or green to entice other birds). Then hang the birdhouse from a tree or wire with the opening away from the wind, and watch for your new tenants!

MORE BIRDHOUSE-BUILDING BASICS

You can also make sturdy wood birdhouses to attract many different kinds of birds. Ask an adult to help you get started (for plans for different birdhouse designs, check with the National Audubon Society or a local bird or conservation group in your area). Then put your beginning woodworking skills to use!

Here are some points to keep in mind when planning a birdhouse:

- Use untreated wood; chemical fumes can harm birds.
- Galvanized screws and nails resist rust and last longer.
- All houses need ventilation holes near the top.
- Drainage holes are needed on the floor of the house.
- Do not use perches, as these are often used by predators.
- Use a rough surface inside the box so birds can climb out.
- In hot climates, face the houses north or east.

Birdhouses for a Cause

Make birdhouses with a group of friends. Put them up in your neighborhood or donate them to a local park, senior citizens' housing, or community or nature centers. You could also sell birdhouses to raise money for birding and conservation organizations (see pages 85 and 122).

TRY THIS!

Help Threatened Birds in Your Area

Your state Department of Natural Resources, local parks and nature centers, and birding groups have information about birds that have lost their nesting habitats. Choose a bird that's in danger in your area and make a house just the right size (you can find birdhouse plans in library books or on the Internet).

• B U T T E R F L I E S •

Create a Butterfly Retreat

Butterflies need your help, too. Unfortunately, with the growth of cities and sub-urbs and the loss of wild areas, there is less and less butterfly habitat available. Butterflies need places full of flowering plants where they can sip nectar and specific plants (like milkweed for monarch butterflies) where they can lay their eggs. These beautiful, graceful insects are also threatened in the countryside by harmful sprays used on crops. You can help butterflies survive by growing the plants they need in their habitat. And you don't need a big garden to do it: plants in pots on a patio or deck will help. You can also organize a group to plant a butterfly garden at your school or community center.

what you need

- Garden space, or containers and potting soil

- Tape measure

- Flower seeds or starter plants (see BUTTERFLY PLANTS MENU, page 78)

- Trowel

- Watering can or hose

1 Most butterfly plants grow best in sunshine, so try to find a sunny space to prepare your garden. Measure your garden area and plan it according to the space each plant needs. Pick plants that will grow well in your climate, and plan to group the same kind of plant in clusters to make it easier for butterflies to track down their favorites.

2 Prepare the garden soil or the containers and plant the seeds according to the package directions or transplant the starter plants. Water and care for the plants as they grow. Then keep an eye out for your colorful visitors!

Community Butterfly Bonanza

Here's a way to beautify your community *and* help the butterflies at the same time! Join together with other kids (and adults) and ask for permission to plant a butterfly garden at local libraries, nature centers, parks, schools, community centers, or businesses. Some of the town's businesses might even help you buy seeds, soil, and plants. Plan and plant the garden as a group project, then take turns keeping the garden tended. Post a sign to tell others in the community why the garden is so important and how it helps butterflies by providing them with a habitat.

BuTTeRfLy PLANTS MeNu

Butterflies eat entirely different foods at different times of their lives. Baby caterpillars in their larval life stage munch on leaves, eating maybe just one or two plant types. The caterpillar of the monarch butterfly, for example, eats *only* milkweed leaves: it can't eat anything else! As adults, butterflies sip nectar from flowers.

Munching Plants: These are the baby food for the caterpillars, and also the plants on which butterflies lay their eggs! Different butterflies may eat catnip, chives, dill, fennel, lavender, milkweed (the monarch's favorite), mint, nettles, parsley, sunflower, and thistles.

Sipping Plants: Some plants adult butterflies will seek out for nectar are asters, butterfly plant, cosmos, marigolds, milkweed flowers, nasturtium, petunias, snapdragons, sunflowers, sweet peas, and zinnias.

TRY THIS!
Look for Seeds

When flowers begin to drop their petals, seeds can be found. Pick the flower heads and let them dry. As the seeds dry, they will loosen and fall out. Place the seeds in envelopes labeled with the flower's name. Now you have seeds to plant next spring!

A Milkweed Wildspot for Monarchs!

If you've ever seen the beautiful orange, black, and white-spotted monarch butterfly flit past you on a summer day, you know how marvelous the monarch is. Monarchs lay their white eggs on the undersides of milkweed leaves — it's the only plant they can use! The tiny caterpillar that hatches from the egg eats the milkweed leaves until it is large enough to spin a cocoon-like *chrysalis,* where it goes through a magical process called *metamorphosis* and changes into a beautiful butterfly!

You can help the monarch by making sure there is plenty of milkweed around. Scout out milkweed plants at construction sites and other areas that are being developed, and ask permission to move them to your yard or school before the plants are destroyed. You can also gather milkweed seeds from wild plants and tend your home-grown patch in a planter or in a small sunny spot. With your help, and the help of other kids like you, the monarchs' milkweed habitat will survive, and so will the monarchs!

MONARCH WATCH

Join with other kids across the continent to help monitor monarch populations and their habitats. The Monarch Watch group (www.monarchwatch.org) is dedicated to helping the monarch butterfly, and it can use your help! (See page 64 for more nature counts that count on kids like you.)

• ENDANGERED • • ANIMALS •

Have you heard of the olingo, marbled cat, black-footed ferret, or ruffed lemur? These animals are all threatened because of hunting and habitat destruction. (An animal that is *threatened* means that it has so few members left in its population that it is in danger of becoming *extinct,* or lost forever from our planet — like the dodo bird and the dinosaurs — unless immediate action is taken.) You can get the word out and help others care about these and other fascinating animals that share our world.

Make Model Animals

Make endangered animal models to share with others. People will enjoy your creations while learning about the endangered animals on our planet. Include name cards with a few interesting facts and photographs with each animal. Display the animals and information at your local library, share them with younger kids at your school, or give them as gifts. You and your friends could even help organize an Endangered Animal Day, and each bring different animals you have made to show others.

what you need

- Books or Internet information about endangered animals
- Air-drying clay, in a variety of colors
- Toothpicks
- Glue

1 Look for information and photos of endangered or threatened animals in the books or on the Internet. Use the information to choose animals you would like to tell others about.

2 Create models of the animals from the clay. Use a toothpick to add textures and details.

3 Glue on any extra features as necessary to create your animals.

TRY THIS!
Create a Diorama

Use a shoe box to create a diorama for your clay animal. Include all the things in the model habitat that your animal needs to live comfortably.

ENDANGERED-ANIMAL ACTION PLAN

Organize an Endangered Animal Day with other kids (see KIDS JOIN TOGETHER, page 109). Each of you could bring different clay animals you have made (see page 80) to show others at a library, school, or other community gathering place. Make and play ANIMAL ANTICS and put on an endangered-animals puppet show or write a song to educate others about threatened animals. Use ideas from the "HELP THE ANIMALS" FAIR (see page 85) to raise money for organizations that support endangered species.

Animal Survival Game

Create a board game in which endangered animals are the main characters. Playing pieces can be made from clay (see MAKE MODEL ANIMALS, page 80) or from cardboard. Learning and fun go together when you play a game created by you!

what you need

- Scissors
- Cardboard (from cereal boxes or larger boxes)
- Masking tape
- Pencil
- Animal playing pieces (see MAKE MODEL ANIMALS, page 80, or make playing pieces from cardboard scraps)
- Books or Internet information about endangered animals
- Acrylic paint and paintbrushes
- Paper scraps
- Glue
- Black marker
- 3" x 5" (7.5 x 12.5 cm) index cards, cut in half so they measure 3" x 2½" (7.5 x 6 cm)
- Dice

the setup

1 Cut a panel from a large appliance box or tape together panels from cereal boxes to make a game board the size you would like. Sketch a path on your board that the animals need to travel. Divide the path into squares big enough for the playing pieces.

2 Design where the animals are, what they are traveling toward, and what they must pass through on the way. Maybe the path could be traveling away from destroyed homes to a healthy habitat. What kind of place would the animals need to live in? A rain forest, grassy plain, or a clean lake? (Research to find out if you don't know.) What is missing from where they are trying to survive now? Draw that scene at the Start. The animals could go through cities, polluted rivers, garbage heaps and landfills, and over concrete highways or around industrial centers and airports. Maybe they'll pass through jungles, over rivers, across deserts, or around mountains to the habitat they need.

3 Paint over your pencil drawings with bright colors. Let dry.

4 Use paper scraps to make trees, buildings, hills, and other features that you can glue on to pop up from your game board.

5 Use a black marker to darken in the pathway. Add a picture symbol on some of the spaces as a mark showing when a player takes a card.

6 Use the index cards to create game cards by writing events that could either help or hinder the animals' journey. Add the consequence. Use books and other resources for ideas that make sense with the animals you chose as playing pieces.

Hear elephants trumpeting at water hole. Move to closest water source.

Stormy weather causes you to seek shelter. Go back to the nearest cave.

Ripe mangos give you energy. Run ahead 6 spaces.

Outrun predator. Roll dice again.

to play

Place animal playing pieces at the starting space. Take turns rolling dice and moving forward along the path. Choose cards when landing on the special picture spaces. Read the card aloud and follow the directions. The first player to get to the end of the path wins.

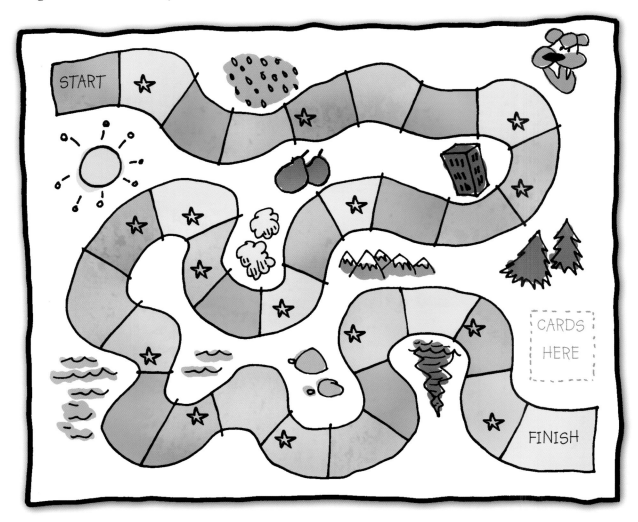

MORE FUN!   Make extra games!

Cover different endangered animals in each game. Share your games with others at libraries or schools (see ENDANGERED-ANIMAL ACTION PLAN, page 82), or sell them at a "HELP THE ANIMALS" FAIR (see facing page).

KIDS CARE TOGETHER

"Help the Animals" Fair

Celebrate and raise money for animal causes with a fair to share your concern and love for animals. You and your friends can sell tickets and items to make money for your favorite animal organizations or for funds for future projects. It's a great way to give out information to help people learn about caring for pets and wildlife, and it's lots of fun for you as well!

what you need

- Card tables for booths (page 119)
- Change box
- Paper tickets (handmade or computer designed)
- Extras: animal decorations, signs, balloons, ribbons, posters, table coverings
- A collection of animal-friendly homemade items to sell, including any of the following:

    Handmade pet toys (pages 32, 35, 39, 43 and 44)

    Dog biscuits (page 47)

    Pet collars (page 56)

    Pet pillows (page 42)

    Animal Survival Game (page 82)

    Bird feeders (page 69)

    Birdhouses (page 72)

    Window art (page 67)

    Bookmarks (page 117)

    Flyers or booklets (page 117)

1 Brainstorm what your group would like to make to sell at the fair and ideas for entertainment. Will you have a pet talent show, set up a booth to make animal-art T-shirts (see page 106 for T-shirt decorating how-to), or host a dog wash (see page 49)? How will you inform fairgoers about your animal concerns? Will you give out information on posters, flyers, or bookmarks?

2 Decide on where you might like to hold your fair (a school? local park? someone's big backyard?), and a possible day that would work for everyone involved. Once you have an idea of what you want to do, enlist the help of an adult. You'll need permission for using any public site, such as a park or school, and you'll need parental or guardian permission for everyone involved in the planning. You might want to write up your idea to present to school officials or the local town board.

Pass for One
Animal Friends Fair
Saturday, June 26
at 226 Forest Street
Booths! Crafts! Games!

3 Once you've decided on a date and place for the fair, make tickets from paper slips or by using a computer. Sell tickets or give them away for free.

4 On the morning of the event, set up your fair. Take turns with your friends staffing the various booths or tables.

KIDS CARE ABOUT THE ENVIRONMENT

Reuse! Reduce! Recycle! These three simple steps can help protect the environment — and *you* can help make them happen! Using less and reusing what we have helps save forests and natural habitats from destruction, and it also means less air and water pollution and less waste. Make a difference by helping people follow the three "Rs." Help save trees by making cloth shopping bags to use instead of paper or plastic bags. Make one-of-a-kind recycling bins to help people remember to collect paper, cans, and other recyclables rather than simply tossing them in the trash (which will then end up in a landfill). Conserve water by collecting rainwater to help trees and other plants grow. Teach others about being environmentally responsible by making earth-friendly cleanup kits that use only safe cleaning solutions that won't harm plants and animals — or you! Turn old T-shirts into EARTH SHIRTS that spread the word about caring for our planet. Every action you take to protect the environment shows that you care. And that is something you can be proud of!

Creature Collectors

Everyone knows that recycling is a good idea, but people don't always make the effort to do it. Throwing something in the garbage just seems easier to some folks. Part of that could be simply because they haven't created designated areas for recyclables, so everything gets dumped in the trash. You can help the people in your household and classroom make recycling part of their everyday habits by making eye-catching collection bins for recyclable materials. At first people may participate just for the fun of it, but with practice they will begin to make the environmentally friendly choice to recycle. Help everyone join in the "feeding" fun!

What you need

- Large cardboard boxes or plastic containers
- Glue
- Recycled materials
- Tempera paint
- Paintbrushes

1 Choose a box or container that is large enough to collect paper, cans, plastic, or glass bottles. (It's a good idea to make a separate box for materials that need to be recycled separately and also one for returnables.)

2 Design each box so it looks like a weird creature or monster. Glue on recycled materials for silly features: jar lids make shiny eyes, a cardboard tube can be a long nose, and scrunched newspaper makes some wild hair!

I EAT CANS

3 Paint the boxes with bright colors to attract attention. Add words like "RECYCLE PAPER HERE!" or "I EAT CANS!" to let everyone know what goes where.

4 Find a good place for your boxes where they will be used (get permission first before you set up your creature collectors). They should be out of the way but easily visible. Place them by a trash can to help train people to recycle instead of throwing items away.

5 On recycling day, help sort and take out the items your creature collectors have been fed.

Recycling Rascals for All!

Make lots of containers for all the classrooms in a school or for organizations or meeting places. You can even help coordinate how the recyclables will be picked up. Maybe you and some friends can volunteer to be on recycling duty to help out. Recycling is hard to ignore when your group shares these rascally receptacles!

ReCYCLe OR ReTuRNS

Not all places have the same recycling and returnable regulations. In some locations, for example, you can put everything that is recyclable (glass, plastic, paper, cardboard) in one bin. That makes it really easy. In other places, a lot of the materials need to be presorted into bins with glass, bins with cans, bins with plastic, and bins with newspaper. Some states accept returnable bottles and cans (you return them to a store and you get 5 cents, 10 cents, and in some places, 15 cents for each one returned).

Check out your recycling rules before you get started. Call or visit the web site of your local solid waste district for a copy of what is expected in your location.

TRY THIS!
Earn Money Returning
If your state has a bottle deposit law, you can get paid for the returnable cans and bottles that you find. Just take them to any store that carries those same items, and you'll get to pocket the deposit.

GIVE A HELPING HAND
Recycling can be hard for older people or others who are ill, especially if the items need to be taken out to the curb or down steps. That's where you come in! Offer to do the weekly recycling for someone in your apartment, on your block, or in your neighborhood. You will be helping that person, which is always appreciated, and helping the environment, too!

Game Time!

Go on a Scavenger Hunt for Recycled Materials

Make up a scavenger hunt that helps people learn about recycling while having fun hunting and searching. Or, with some adult helpers, organize teams to search for recyclable materials along quiet roadways and in parks in your town. The team that finds the most recyclables wins.

Reduce, Reuse, Recycle Board Game

On a large cardboard playing board, draw a winding path that twists and turns through a town to the local landfill. Each player receives cards with pictures of items that can be reused, returned, or recycled. Players toss the single die to see how many steps they move forward. Then they look at their cards. Players need to find a way to dispose of their items before reaching the landfill. Some spaces may send a player to the store to buy another item — *oh no!* The player reaching the landfill with the fewest objects wins. (See ANIMAL SURVIVAL GAME, page 82, for more directions on making board games.)

TEACH WHAT YOU KNOW

Older kids (like you) can help younger children learn how to recycle by playing this game. Once recycling becomes a habit for them, they can teach their friends, and if you keep passing on the recycling message, there will be less garbage all around.

THE SETUP. Gather a pillowcase, four cartons, and the following small household items: empty plastic milk jug, beverage bottles, a newspaper, a shirt or pair of shoes that is in good condition, and something to represent kitchen scraps, like a banana peel or orange rind. Mark the cartons with the words RECYCLE, REUSE, COMPOST, and GIVE AWAY, and also draw an appropriate picture on the outside of the container (for kids who don't read yet). To make it even more fun, use mini CREATURE COLLECTORS (see page 88). Line up the cartons in a row.

TO PLAY. Give the younger child a pillowcase full of the "garbage" that you have selected. Explain what each carton is used for; then invite the child to play. Ask her to place each item from the pillowcase into the correct bin. If she chooses the wrong container, make a funny sound that will signal that she should choose another container. Reward correct efforts with applause!

TRY THIS!

Teach Adults, Too!

The fact is that a lot of adults today did not grow up with the idea of recycling. People just didn't know how important it is to recycle back then, but you can help them learn! Set up a recycling center in your house (asking first where it would be best to put it). Then make a poster showing what can go in each container. Tell your whole household how important this is, and ask for everyone's help. Once the adults realize that recycling is something we all need to do, they'll get the hang of it and recycling will become as easy for them as it is for you.

PLEASE RECYCLE

ALUMINUM CANS   STEEL CANS   PLASTIC

"Use it up, wear it out, make it do, or do without!"

Have you ever heard this old saying? It might have been used when your grandparents, or *their* grandparents, were growing up, and it applies to how we all should live today as well. Back then, it was mostly spoken about as a way to save money rather than preserving natural resources. Do you think you can live this way today to save both the environment and some money?

Rather than always buying new things as styles change, try using what you have, or improvise by changing something you already own to make it work for a new purpose. You'll find all sorts of ideas for reusing items in the pages that follow. When you want to buy something new, it's good to ask, "Do I really need this?" You may just decide that you can "make do" with what you have already, or that you can do without. You'll be saving money by not buying something you don't really need, and you'll also help the environment in the long run by not supporting excessive production of items that use nature's resources.

Bag It!

Sew yourself a cloth shopping bag that can be used again and again. When asked at the store if you want "paper or plastic," you can say proudly, "Neither one, thank you!" and pull out your homemade cloth bag. You'll save trees, and the landfill won't pile up with unnecessary waste.

What you need

- Strong fabric (canvas, denim, twill), 15" x 30" (37.5 x 75 cm)
- Needle and thread, or sewing machine (to use with adult help)
- Twill tape, 2" x 24" (5 x 60 cm)
- Newspaper (optional)
- Fabric paint or marker (optional)

1 Fold the fabric in half, with the "right" (or good) sides together, so the short sides meet at the top.

2 Sew a seam along the sides. (See TAKE A STITCH, page 24).

3 Turn the bag right side out. Fold the top edge and sew in place. Sew the twill tape to the top sides of the bag as shown to make a shoulder strap.

4 Decorate the bag with fabric paint or markers if you like. (First fill the bag with flat newspapers so the paint or ink doesn't leak through.)

Make and sell cloth bags to raise awareness of recycling, and donate the money you make to an environmental organization (see page 123 for some ideas). Add a "Save a Tree!" slogan to decorate the bag, or come up with your own slogan and design. Ask permission to sell bags at food cooperatives, farmers' markets, and grocery stores.

• Overpackaging ALert! •

Now that you're using cloth bags, do you notice other wasteful ways? Fancy, individually wrapped items that you find in stores are not the best use of Mother Nature's resources. Most often, the overpackaging is designed to be thrown away after the product is opened, so all of that paper, plastic, and cardboard are *used only once!* Paper uses up trees, and the papermaking process produces pollutants. Most plastic is not biodegradable, so it gets dumped in landfills, where it sits for a very long time. And get this: the amount you pay for that product includes what it costs to make that packaging, too!

You can make a difference by buying products that come in recyclable, reusable, or refillable containers whenever possible. And you can decide *not* to buy the overpackaged products! You might even write or email the company and tell it that you won't be buying any of its products until it cuts back on the packaging and avoids using plastics, because you care about the future of our planet.

At the grocery store, suggest to your adult family members that they bring their own containers and use the bulk bins for rice, flour, nuts, and dried fruits. Maybe your family can even join a co-op that buys products in bulk without all the fancy wrappings.

Then, when you need to wrap a package for that next holiday or birthday, make your own recycled wrapping! (See page 96 for some ideas, and then come up with your own designs.)

Leaf-Print Gift Wrap

Gift wrap is fun to make, and it shows the gift recipients that you care about them and the environment! Any present wrapped in homemade gift wrap is more meaningful just because you took the time to create the wrapping yourself. Use your leaf-print wrapping paper for any holiday or occasion.

What you need

- Leaves, various shapes and sizes
- Old phone book and several heavy books
- Old newspapers
- Acrylic paint, variety of colors, in separate bowls or containers
- Rolls of brown or white recycled paper, cut into 20" (50 cm) sheets
- Paintbrushes
- Ribbon or string

1 Place the leaves between the pages of the phone book. Stack the other books on top of the phone book to press the leaves as flat as possible.

2 Cover your work surface with newspaper. Arrange the paints and paper sheets on top of the newspaper.

3 Using one color at a time, spread paint over the vein side of the leaves and then press the leaves in patterns or randomly onto the paper. Allow the paper to dry completely.

4 To store the wrapping paper, roll three or more sheets together and tie the roll closed with string or ribbon.

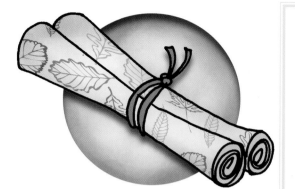

Gift Wrap for a Cause

Gift wrap is a great item to sell for an important environmental cause. Use a colorful raffia ribbon to tie the rolls of gift wrap together, and then decide on a price for each bundle. Sell your homemade wrapping paper to family, friends, and neighbors, and be sure to let them know how the money will be used.

MORE FUN! Make rainbow gift-wrap bags

Jazz up your gift giving with these colorful gift-wrap bags. Use bags of various sizes — grocery to lunch bag or smaller — so that you have a variety of sizes to choose from when wrapping.

Start by painting the bottom of the bags any color you like. When the bottom is dry, flatten the bag and paint horizontal stripes on it. Do one side and let it dry, then do the other side. It will take only a few minutes for the paint to dry in the sun, or you can use a hair dryer (with adult help) to make the drying go more quickly. You can vary the sizes of the painted lines and even blend the edges of the paints together. If you want true "rainbow" colors, apply the paints in this order: red, orange, yellow, green, blue, and at the top, purple. Choose some yarn to match the bags so that you can tie the top closed after the gift is placed inside.

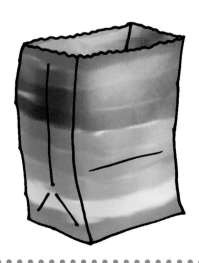

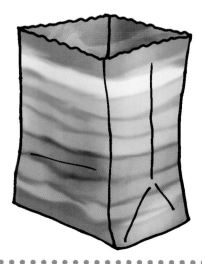

Better-Than-New Toy Shop

Do you have a few perfectly good toys that just need a little fixing or some fresh paint? Join with others to spruce up used toys to donate to those in need (see page 25) or to sell to help make money for a cause that is important to you and your friends. By reusing the toys, you'll also help the environment by keeping them out of the trash.

What you need

- Gently used toys (collected from friends and classmates)
- Box
- Acrylic paint
- Paintbrushes
- Rags
- Soap
- Dishpan
- Tape
- Glue
- Sewing supplies
- Tools (as needed)

1 Sort the toys, placing any that are good-as-new in a box to be sold or donated.

2 Sort toys that can be cleaned or fixed into three groups: those that need cleaning, need painting, and need mending.

3 Hold a work session to get the toys in good condition. Ask an adult to help you with any repair tasks that are more complex than washing, gluing, sewing, or adding a coat of paint.

TOYS FOR SALE

If you decide to sell the toys for a good cause, plan on a date and time for the sale, as well as a work schedule and adult supervision. Advertise the date, time, place, and reason for the sale with posters, bookmarks, or flyers (see pages 117 and 118).

Before the day of the sale, mark prices on the toys with pieces of masking tape. Make sure you keep prices low enough to give children a chance to get a good deal!

On the day of the sale, set up tables and group similar kinds of toys together. Decide what task each person in the group will do during the sale before the customers arrive. Some of the group's members will need to help collect money and make change, while others can keep track of sales, stock tables, and help customers. Then put on a smile and get ready to greet your customers!

Safety First!

Repair and refurbish only simple toys that don't have electrical cords or electronics. Don't try to fix toys that have electric cords or are powered by batteries or computer chips.

Earth-Friendly Cleanup Kit

Incredible as it may sound, sometimes keeping things clean is actually bad for your health. Many of the products sold for housecleaning are more toxic than they need to be, making them unhealthy for people and for the environment. Ammonia, for instance, gives off fumes that aren't good for humans to breathe in, and the phosphorus in detergents can cause pollution in water supplies. And these polluting products cost a lot to buy, too. Luckily, you don't have to use them at all: There are plenty of make-it-yourself cleaners that do the job just as well as the advertised products, and they won't pollute the air, water, or soil. But don't take our word for it: Create your own EARTH-FRIENDLY CLEANUP KIT and put it to the test!

What you need

- Plastic bottles or canning jars with lids, washed well
- Baking soda
- Cream of tartar
- Salt
- Lemon juice
- Olive oil
- Vinegar
- Labels
- Permanent marker
- Small pails (ice cream buckets work great and are recyclable!)
- Old towels, washed and cut into rags

1 Use the recipes on page 101 to make your earth-friendly cleaning supplies.

2 Store the mixtures in the containers.

3 Label each container with the following information:

> Earth-Friendly Cleaning
> Product Name:
> Ingredients:
> Uses:
> Date:

4 Place all the containers in a pail along with a few clean rags.

Earth-Friendly Ingredients

Please ask permission before using these products on your household furniture or appliances.

Kitchen Cleaner

Use to clean sinks, appliances, countertops, and other surfaces.

> ¼ cup (50 ml) baking soda
> 4 cups (1 L) water

Sink and Drain Cleaner

Scrub with a paste of this mixture, leaving overnight in the sink if needed to remove stains. Pour ¼ cup (60 ml) of the mixture down the drain once a week. Run a slow stream of hot water afterward to wash it down the pipes.

> 1 cup (250 ml) baking soda
> ¼ cup (60 ml) cream of tartar
> 1 cup (250 ml) salt

Furniture Polish

First, dust the furniture. Then, place a little polish on a rag and rub it into the furniture. Buff with a clean, dry rag.

> ¼ cup (60 ml) lemon juice
> ½ cup (125 ml) olive oil

Window Cleaner

Dampen a rag with the mixture to clean windows.

> 1 cup (250 ml) vinegar
> ¼ cup (60 ml) lemon juice

CLEANUP KITS TO GO

Pack up several of the cleaning kits on pages 100 to 101. Include colorful sponges, clean towels, and an informational pamphlet with nonpolluting cleaning tips. Sell the kits as a fund-raiser to help an environmental cause. You'll raise money and help others become aware of alternative ways to clean that are healthier for people and the environment. (For more on fund-raising basics and a list of organizations that help the environment, see pages 120 to 123.)

NO 'CIDES ALLOWED!

True or false? "Cleaning up" the lawn (not including raking) around your house can harm the environment. True! Pesticides and insecticides, used to kill unwanted critters and insects that live in lawns, will also kill many harmless animals. They are dangerous for people as well. Herbicides that are used to kill weeds in lawns and gardens are also bad news for people, pets, and many other creatures. One big problem is that these chemicals eventually make their way into water supplies, causing pollution far away from the backyard where they were first applied. Do your part to help the environment by making your backyard a pesticide-, herbicide-, and insecticide-free area!

Sprout a Tree

Want to help our planet and all of its people and creatures stay healthy? Well then, grow a tree! And take a big, deep breath as you plant. After all, trees help keep the air healthy by taking in the carbon dioxide that we breathe out and releasing oxygen that we can breathe in. It's all pretty neat, isn't it? When a tree is cut down, it's like taking away a breath of fresh air. Trees also provide shade from the sun, serve as homes and provide food for wild birds and animals, and are beautiful to look at. A tree is a friend for life! Unfortunately, every day more and more forests are being destroyed all over the planet as a result of industry, new houses and stores, roads, and other development. You can help slow this trend by planting trees wherever you live and helping to care for them until they are sturdy enough to make it on their own.

What you need

- Tree seeds
- Paper towels
- Plastic sandwich bag
- Box or other container
- Flowerpots
- Potting soil
- Trowel
- Stake or section of wire fencing

1 Look for maple "helicopters," acorns, pinecones, or other types of tree seeds. Notice how different each type of seed is.

2 Wrap each kind of seed in damp paper towels and place in the plastic bag. Close the bag loosely so some air is still able to enter the bag. Place the bag in a dark place, such as a box. Check on the seeds each day and keep the toweling damp.

OAK

HICKORY

ELM

MAPLE

3 When a seed forms a sprout, plant the seed in a pot filled with potting soil. (It's a good idea to plant several pots of each type of seed for a better chance that one will grow strong and survive.) Place the pot in the sunlight (but out of the direct hot sun) and water the seedling as the soil becomes dry. Do not overwater!

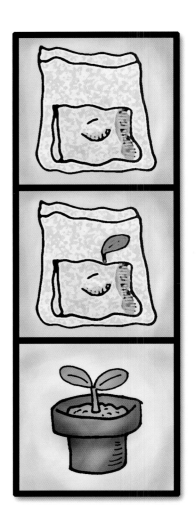

4 Once the seedlings have a second set of leaves (called *true leaves*), you can plant them outside. Consult with an adult as to the best place for your trees (remember, they may grow tall!), and then dig a small hole in the ground for each seedling. Pour water in the hole first so that the roots will get a good drink. Then, carefully tip the small tree from its pot, and place it in the hole. Cover the roots with soil, carefully packing it down as you go. Place a stake near each tree or some wire fencing around it so that you can easily see where it is — you don't want your new trees to get stepped on or mowed down.

5 Continue to care for your trees as they grow. Water them through the summer and fall, mulch around the roots, and they will reward you with green leaves and shade for years to come!

Hold a tree ceremony

Planting a tree is a special act of kindness to the earth.

Hold a tree-planting ceremony to honor the life of your tree and its importance to the ecology of the planet. Take your picture next to the tree, and then, just for fun, take it every year around Memorial Day weekend. You'll be amazed at how you and the tree change and grow every year! Which one of you is growing the straightest and tallest? Trees are often planted to celebrate someone's life, and they are used as a symbol of friendship and peace, too. Plant a tree together with a friend or group of friends and dedicate it to peace, wildlife, a pet, a special person, or the environment.

TENDER CARE FOR CITY TREES

City trees offer welcome shade, and they release oxygen in the very spot where a breath of fresh air is most needed. But living in the city is hard on even the sturdiest trees. Often the soil around a city tree has been neglected and is so tightly packed that it offers little nourishment. You can help a city tree stay alive and healthy by giving it a regular checkup and attention.

Soil check. If the soil is tightly packed, use an old fork, spoon, or garden trowel to gently loosen the top 2 or 3 inches (5 to 7.5 cm) of soil. (Don't dig any deeper, or you might damage the tree's roots.)

Mulching time. Once the soil is loosened, you can feed the tree. Sprinkle compost, composted (not fresh!) manure, peat moss, ground-up leaves, or wood chips around the tree as mulch. The mulch layer will protect the tree during the winter, and come spring, the materials will break down to help nourish the roots.

Water, please! Unless it has just rained, your adopted tree will need a drink. City trees get especially thirsty with the heat from pavement, buildings, and road surfaces. Give the tree about 6 gallons (23 L) of water two times a week. It's best to water in the late afternoon when the sun is lower in the sky. Be especially attentive to the tree's needs in the late summer and fall, when there is less rainfall.

Your tree will thank you for your care with its shade and beauty for many years to come!

Earth Shirts

Share an environmental message or your love of nature by making and wearing Earth T-shirts designed by you!

What you need

- White paper
- Markers
- Solid-colored T-shirts (used shirts are perfect!)
- Pencil
- Fabric paints
- Miscellaneous decorations: fabric glue, fabric scraps, fabric glitter paint, puffy paint, photo transfers

1 Plan your T-shirt design on paper first. Think about what type of environmental message you would like to share. Do you want to draw trees, water, animals, or the whole planet? Experiment with drawings and colors until you find a design that pleases you most. Also think about where the drawing should be placed on the shirt and decide on the best way to state your message.

2 Draw your design on the shirt with a pencil. Paint over the designs and letters with fabric paints. Add other decorations as desired. Make several earth shirts with different designs and messages.

TRY THIS!
Photo-Transfer Shirts

Do you have a great photo of an animal or special natural area? Use it for an environmental message! Photographs can be placed on T-shirts with a photo-transfer kit (available from office supply stores). The photographs are printed from a computer onto special paper. The transfer is then ironed (with adult help) onto the shirt.

Environ-Group Tees

Design a logo for your group and make T-shirts that display your cause!

Make extra tees in varied sizes. Then, set up a booth (see page 119) to sell the tees to raise money *and* raise awareness of the environment.

Turn Over
A New Leaf
and
GET GREEN!

Organize a "Save the Earth" Festival

Put on a festival to celebrate our planet on Earth Day (April 22), or any day. Organize games, play music, demonstrate earth-friendly ideas, and set up booths to share information. Games might include tossing plastic bottles into recycling bins, or a contest to see who can make the tallest tower from aluminum cans. Give away tree seedlings as prizes. Sell items to raise money for conservation projects. You might want to include:

BIRD FEEDERS (page 69)
CREATURE COLLECTORS (page 88)
CLOTH SHOPPING BAGS (page 94)
LEAF-PRINT GIFT WRAP (page 96)
EARTH-FRIENDLY CLEANUP KITS (page 100)
EARTH SHIRTS (page 106)

Choose a task or two that people can help with, such as picking up litter in a neighborhood park, mulching and watering trees, or planting trees at a school or public building. Most of all, celebrate the outdoors and the natural world all around you. Take a walk, smell the flowers, notice birds and wildlife, and treasure all that Mother Nature has to offer! With your help, it will be here for others to enjoy, too!

KIDS JOIN TOGETHER!

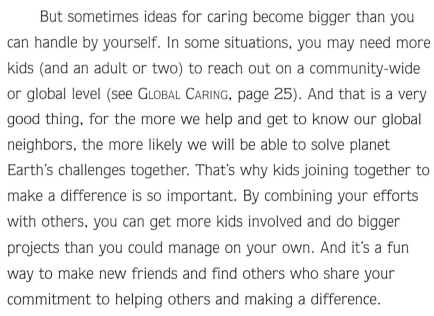

You've learned many ways to care for people, pets, wildlife, and the environment. Good for you! You have accomplished a lot already and should feel very proud of yourself and the help you've offered. As you've discovered, many acts of caring can be done right at home, or in your town or neighborhood, by yourself. By helping, you are making a difference — and your involvement shows that you care.

But sometimes ideas for caring become bigger than you can handle by yourself. In some situations, you may need more kids (and an adult or two) to reach out on a community-wide or global level (see GLOBAL CARING, page 25). And that is a very good thing, for the more we help and get to know our global neighbors, the more likely we will be able to solve planet Earth's challenges together. That's why kids joining together to make a difference is so important. By combining your efforts with others, you can get more kids involved and do bigger projects than you could manage on your own. And it's a fun way to make new friends and find others who share your commitment to helping others and making a difference.

Here you will learn how to form a group, pick a project, get organized, and keep the activity interesting and purposeful as you work side by side to help promote a cause or meet a need. Educate others about the global or community need you are working on by using flyers, games, skits, and informational booths. Fund-raising plans will help your group collect money for global caring projects and to make donations to other helping organizations. Look for the KIDS CARE TOGETHER logo throughout the book for ideas that can be done with a small or larger group. The actions of kids like you, caring together, are sure to make the world better for many.

· JOINING · TOGETHER ·

The first thing you need in order to form a group of caring kids is — more kids! Don't worry if you have only a few people. A group can start with just one or two other people. Starting small is often the best way, as it is easier to become organized and focused on the task you select. After you get moving on a project, your group will grow as others become interested in what you are doing.

A caring group of kids can become an after-school or even in-school project. Ask your teacher for ideas about forming an organization or a kids' club. Scouts, community youth organizations, churches, synagogues, and library activity centers might also be a place to start a kids' action group.

Here are a few tips to keep in mind:

· Start small

Fewer members are easier to organize, and you may be able to meet in your homes. Your group can always grow, as needed, or ask for volunteers for bigger projects.

· Branch out

Do include kids who are interested, even if you don't know them well. Kids do not all need to know each other, or to be best friends, to be in a group. Maybe you or others in your club know friends from different schools or neighborhoods. That's just fine! You will all get to know one another as you work together. *Don't* try to include those who don't want to join. They may become sincerely interested once they see what you accomplish, but until then, they might take away from the rest of the group.

· Combine your interests

Include kids who have different kinds of interests, talents, and personalities. Is someone you know really interested in creating art? He might like making posters to promote your cause. Does another person have a flair for words and writing? She might be interested in writing about your project for the newspaper or creating a pamphlet. Is another person good at inspiring others? She might be a natural leader. And someone who is good at organizing things will help the whole group stay on track! The more combined skills and interests the group has, the easier it will be to get the work done.

Pardon me, but would any of you be interested in helping me with a project?

FINDING SPONSORS:
ADULTS NEEDED!

Before starting a big project, you'll need to have adult support. An adult sponsor is someone who volunteers to do the things you need help with. He or she can help you organize your efforts with other groups or connect you with organizations you want to contribute to. Sponsors can be parents, neighbors, relatives, teachers, or youth leaders.

Discuss your group's goals and ideas with your adult sponsors and explain how you will need their help. They might also have good ideas about how you can get started helping others.

Of course, all parents and guardians should know when you are involved in a big project. There are many times when you will want to do planning and projects on your own, but you should always tell the adults in your life *what* you are doing, *where* you will be, *who* you are going to be with and *when* you are planning an event or meeting.

TRY THIS!
Share the "Who, What, Where, and When"

It seems to be a fact of life that when the adults in your life know what you are doing and with whom, and where, they are much more supportive, and life is better for all of those in your household. Letting adults know what you are doing does not mean they are going to "take over;" in fact, just the opposite is true. Knowing you are safe allows them to focus on other things in their lives, without worrying about you. So try it! Tell adults about your after-school clubs and groups, and watch things smooth out at home. Your whole family will thank you!

There's so much to help with — the problem is deciding where to begin! So the first order of business will be to choose an area your group wants to focus on. Does your group want to help hurricane victims? Work for clean water? Assist the elderly? Educate people about caring for the environment? There are so many choices, and so many different ways to contribute to a cause!

1. Agree as a group on a focus.

Does your group want to focus on one specific area of caring such as animal care? Or, would your group prefer to have a wider range of activities? Maybe your group wants to be an animal-care group that can still respond to global emergencies, such as rescuing animals in a war-torn area.

2. Share ideas, giving everyone a chance to speak.

You might want to write all the ideas on a chalkboard or piece of paper. After each person has had a chance to speak and suggest something, read the list back to the group and decide together on one idea to begin with. Keep in mind that some ideas need immediate action, such as helping people after a major flood. Remember, you can always go back to the suggestion list and work on other ideas, when there isn't an emergency.

3. Choose a specific activity or project.

Once an area of concentration has been selected, keep in mind your group members' interests, skills, and desire to help. Decide if your goal is to raise funds to give to a larger organization such as the United Way, or if your goal is to do hands-on helping such as volunteering where needed. You might want to start with a simple activity like volunteering at a food bank (see page 28), making milk-jug bird feeders (see page 69), or putting together welcome kits (see page 19). Or, maybe you are ready to jump into a bigger project. Sometimes a situation is so urgent that we feel we must take action right away! In either case, your group will need an action plan (see page 114).

4. Set realistic goals.

A lot of your efforts are going to involve hard work and long hours. Set realistic goals so that you can gauge how well you are doing. Having goals is a great motivator, too. Your group can measure its progress and can all pull together to accomplish what you set out to do. When you achieve your goal, you can celebrate that great feeling of completing a project. Should you not be able to attain your goal, it is good to gather together and analyze what went well and what could have been done differently. Maybe your goal was unrealistic, or maybe you needed more people working with you. Whatever the reason, celebrate your good, sincere efforts to help.

READY ... SET ... ACTION!

A plan of action helps your group stay focused and get things done. Lists and charts help people organize what they need to do. If you have someone in your group who enjoys organizing things, then this is the job for that person. Here are ideas for getting organized:

- Divide up jobs with to-do lists.
- Make sure everyone has something to do.
- List supplies that each person will gather for a project.
- Use a chart or calendar to schedule meetings.
- Make a list of everyone's phone numbers, addresses, and e-mail. Make sure everyone has a copy.
- Keep track of what still needs to be done by making new lists as the project continues.

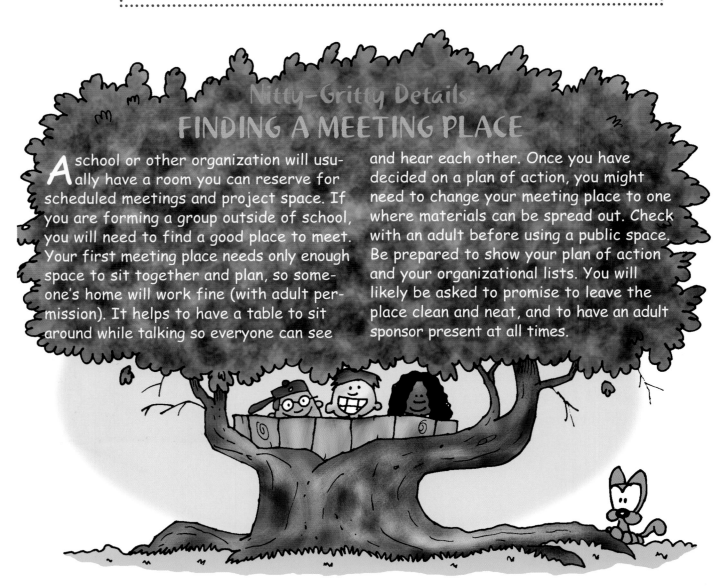

Nitty-Gritty Details
FINDING A MEETING PLACE

A school or other organization will usually have a room you can reserve for scheduled meetings and project space. If you are forming a group outside of school, you will need to find a good place to meet. Your first meeting place needs only enough space to sit together and plan, so someone's home will work fine (with adult permission). It helps to have a table to sit around while talking so everyone can see and hear each other. Once you have decided on a plan of action, you might need to change your meeting place to one where materials can be spread out. Check with an adult before using a public space. Be prepared to show your plan of action and your organizational lists. You will likely be asked to promise to leave the place clean and neat, and to have an adult sponsor present at all times.

Names for a Cause!

A name gives your group an identity and helps its members feel connected. A group name also helps when you are advertising fund-raising events and projects, as the more you accomplish, the more people will recognize your group as reliable and hard-working. Brainstorm ideas for a name, letting everyone make suggestions before taking a vote to choose one that sticks. Names might include where you live and the kinds of projects your group wants to do. The first letters of each word in a group's name can also be used as an *abbreviation*, or if the word is pronounceable, an *acronym*. How about a name like Kansas City Kids Care (KCKC) or the Children's Animal Rescue Project (CARP)? CARP is an acronym because you can pronounce it and because a carp is a fish, the name has meaning related to what the group does. Acronyms are sometimes difficult to come up with, but they are excellent names, because even the initials tell a person what the group is about.

WRITE A SLOGAN!

Slogans are great for letting people know the purpose of your group, and they even help you keep focused on your goals. A good slogan is catchy, easy to remember, and goes right to the main point of your group's existence. Which of these slogans do you think is the best?

Save the Trees!
Stop the Violence!
No More Hungry Children!
A Chicken in Every Pot!
Eat Right to Live Better!

Now *you* write some slogans for your group. Then read all of them and select the one that is the best for what you hope to accomplish. If you want, you can set your slogan to music, in which case you will have a *jingle,* too.

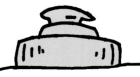

Reaching out is a way to let others know about your group's interests in helping. **The more that people understand the needs of other people, animals, or the environment, the more they can help.** Make a flyer that explains how much water is used in your community with tips on reducing water usage. Help people learn about ways to help feed the hungry by organizing a food-drive scavenger hunt (see page 26). **Teach people to care** about the environment by performing a skit where characters learn about conservation. The more you share what you know about a cause, the more you can involve others in making a difference, too.

Share Your Talents!

You and the others in your group have many skills and talents to help spread your message and get more group members. Kids who like to write can help explain facts and describe ways people can help. Artists add a special flare when designing eye-catching posters, flyers, and bookmarks (see pages 117 and 118). Kids who love music can create songs, play instruments, and sing to make any event more festive (see page 15). Actors in the group will enjoy creating shows and skits that pass the message by performing in other classrooms, at adult organizations, and at youth groups. Others are great at organizing people and materials, working with the public, managing money, and helping events to run smoothly. No matter what each person likes to do, there is a way to use everyone's talents and interests to meet your goals!

There was a young girl, name of Claire,
Who just had to drive everywhere.
Her friends said that she
Could save energy
So now she just walks here & there.

Flyer Fun

A *flyer* is a paper that shares information by using pictures and words, and it is often used to advertise a special event or group need. Flyers can be written, designed, and printed on the computer, or they can be written and designed by hand. Art and photos add interest and make the flyer's message easier to grasp. You'll first need to decide if the flyers will be given or mailed to individuals, displayed on community bulletin boards, or tacked to posts (with permission). That will help you decide if they are to be printed on one side only, or folded (usually in thirds) and printed on both sides.

What do you hope your flyer will do? Do you want people to sign up for something? Contribute food, money, or materials? Join your efforts? Come to a big meeting? If you want people to take an action, you need to make that clear and provide a simple way to do that.

Would you care to know a little more about our local animal shelter?

The Wolf Eel looks like a real sea monster, but is actually quite docile.

Make Bookmarks

A bookmark can include simple slogans as well as facts on a topic that you want other people to know about. For instance, one side might say SAVE THE WHALES with a whale illustration and the other side could include facts about whales and things people can do to help protect them. Your group can also make bookmarks to advertise club events and fund-raisers. Ask permission to give out bookmarks at school libraries, public libraries, and book fairs. Some local bookstores may also agree to hand them out. It's a great way to promote your club's goals and let others know how they can help!

Publicize with Posters

A poster is a simpler, larger version of a flyer that usually summarizes information by using a slogan, has a big drawing or photo on it, and gives the Who, What, Where, When information very clearly. Posters are a great way to let people know about a fund-raising event, such as a dog wash (see page 49), "HELP THE ANIMALS" FAIR (see page 85), or a "save the earth" festival (see page 108). Display them on bulletin boards at schools or youth centers, in windows, and on posts and walls where they are allowed (please get permission first).

Poster Tips:

- Posters should be easy to read and understand without any extra words.

- Plan illustrations to attract attention. Usually one large illustration or photo works best.

- Use large, bold lettering. Consider printing the words in large, bold type from the computer and pasting it to the poster, rather than hand-printing the words.

- Include a contact number or web site for those who have additional questions. Hang your posters about a week before the event.

- Always take down all posters the day after the event. (Save the poster board to use the other side for future posters.)

Set Up a Booth

A booth is a place people visit to gather information such as your flyers (see page 117), sign up to join or participate in the future, or participate in an activity immediately. You can set up a booth at fairs, festivals, and other events or at a local grocery store or town hall with permission. Information booths are a great way for people to learn about your group's purpose. Or, set up an arts and crafts booth where you can share activities such as making EARTH SHIRTS (see page 106), birdhouses (see pages 72 and 74), or pet collars (see page 56). Booths also give your club a place to set up fund-raising events.

Booth Tips:

• Make sure your booth is easy to move and set up. Card tables work great.

• Cover the table with a plain tablecloth that hangs to the ground in front. Attach a poster to the front, publicizing your efforts. Decorate the cloth with additional pictures and words about your group's goals and events.

• Add cardboard signs, balloons, cloth banners, or anything else to make your booth eye-catching, but don't make it cluttered.

• Have a schedule of who will work the booth. You will need at least two group members on hand at all times, and an adult sponsor nearby as well.

• If you plan to give away flyers, be sure they are in good supply and stored neatly under your booth.

• If you plan to collect cash donations, be sure you have a locked money box and that the adult has a large manila folder to empty the cash into frequently. Keep a list of everyone who donates and the amounts given, and be prepared to give each person a receipt.

• FUND-RAISING • FUN •

Raising money is an important part of helping those in need. Money buys medicine, food, seeds for planting, animals to milk, clothes, first-aid supplies, building materials, and farm equipment. When a natural disaster strikes, for example, your group can raise money to send to an aid organization such as the American Red Cross or Habitat for Humanity. They will then arrange for what is most needed and will enable people to receive the specific materials necessary for survival. Your fund-raising money can also go to environmental groups that act to keep our natural world preserved or provide funding for wildlife or pets in need. Perhaps your group feels strongly about saving the endangered rhinoceros. You can reach across the ocean and continents by raising funds to send to an African-wildlife protection fund such as the Wildlife Conservation Society. If helping pets is a favorite cause, your fund-raising efforts can help the local Humane Society chapter or other organizations in your area, or the national chapter.

Look for the KIDS CARE TOGETHER logo in the chapters throughout this book to find ideas for fund-raisers that interest you and your group. Matching your club member's talents and interests is sure to make your fund-raiser a success!

Wheee!

FUND-RAISING IDEAS

There are so many ways to raise money, depending on the cause you are raising it for and how many people are in the group. Look back at the activities in this book to see which ones lend themselves best to raising money. As much as possible, tie your fund-raiser to the purpose, such as having a dog wash (see page 49) to raise money for the Humane Society. Keep in mind that the less money you spend on your fund-raiser, the more money you will raise to donate.

Here are some good ways to raise money. Remember, you will need permission to hold any of these events in a public place and you will also need an adult sponsor.

• **Organize a bake sale.** Arrange to hold it where there will be a lot of people, such as outside the local store on a Friday afternoon or at a soccer or football field the day of the game. Have plenty of cookies, brownies, and cupcakes, as well as cakes and pies, to sell.

• **Hold a holiday wrap at a local mall or at a big store.** Buy the gift wrap at a wholesale price, if possible, and be sure to charge enough to cover the wrap and the ribbon, plus earn a profit on your time and effort. Make and sell your own LEAF-PRINT GIFT WRAP (see page 96), too!

• **Set up a car wash.** Remember while customers are present that you are spraying the cars, not each other! The better job you do cleaning the cars, the more likely people are to tip you with extra money for the cause.

• **Make a product well and then sell it.** Whether you make great bird feeders, knit scarves and hats, or weave wonderful key chains, a handmade item is always a good item for a fund-raiser, as long as it is well made. Be sure to have small bags to put the purchased items in for carrying.

• **Start flower, tree, and herb seeds to sell as young plants.** It is also easy to start Christmas cactus and jade plants from larger plants, and they make wonderful houseplants to sell in green plastic pots.

• **Sell services.** Raking leaves, weeding gardens, pet care (see page 52), shoveling snow, washing windows, reading time with children, and giving computer lessons are all jobs you can do to raise money for a cause.

FUND-RAISING TIPS

• Identify how you are going to raise money. Remember, whatever your fund-raising method, you will need adult sponsors to oversee the project.

• Publicize using posters (page 118) and flyers (page 117) the When, Where, Why, Who, and How of your fund-raiser.

• Be very clear about what you are going to do with the money you raise.

• If you are offering a service, such as raking lawns, be sure to let people know how they can arrange a time for your group to be there. Establish whether you are bringing your own supplies (rakes and leaf bags) or if you expect them to supply them. Confirm the cost for the service and when you expect to be paid.

• If you are selling a product, be sure that it is worth the money charged. Deliver the product on time.

• Call the people who order from you to let them know when you will drop off their order and let them know how much they owe you. Arrange to have an adult with you as you drop off the orders and collect the money.

• Keep collected money in a manila envelope and mark off exactly what each person owes and what he pays with the date. Never mix your own personal cash with the fund-raising cash, and never borrow from the fund-raising money.

• Select someone in the group to be the treasurer to help keep track of the money, using a special notebook to keep a record of expenses and earnings. (Pick someone who is good with math and is very responsible.) By subtracting the expenses for any materials used from what you bring in, you can calculate how much your fund-raiser actually made. Your adult sponsor can safeguard the money as it comes in.

• If you can, send a note or email to the people who bought something or contributed to the fund. Let them know how much money you raised and when you sent a check to the organization. Tell them what the money will be used for.

21, 22, 23...

Check It Out

Research where to send money, being sure that you are sending to those organizations that have an excellent reputation for helping those in need. An adult can help you find places to donate money where it will do the most good, but you will want to do some research yourself to see how much of the money received is actually given to the people or is used to buy what is most urgently needed. Note what percentage of the money received is used for the project directly, and what percentage is used to run the organization and pay the staff. What you want is a very high percentage of the money going to help the cause it was raised to help. The organizations listed here help people, animals, and the environment all over the world. Your fund-raising efforts will help them help others.

Action Against Hunger
www.actionagainsthunger.org

American Red Cross
www.redcross.org

American Refugee Committee
www.arcrelief.org

Animal Welfare Institute
www.awionline.org

Bread for the World
www.bread.org

CARE
www.care.org

Center for Community Change
www.communitychange.org

Climate Crisis
www.climatecrisis.org

Conservation International
www.conservation.org

Direct Relief International
www.directrelief.org

Doctors Without Borders
www.doctorswithoutborders.org

The Elephant Sanctuary
www.elephants.com

Gifts in Kind International
www.giftsinkind.org

The Global Fund for Children
www.globalfundforchildren.org

Guide Dog Foundation for the Blind, Inc.
www.guidedog.org

Habitat for Humanity
www.habitat.org

Heifer International
www.heifer.org

Helen Keller International
www.hki.org

The Humane Society of the U.S.
www.hsus.org

The Hunger Project
www.thp.org

National Alliance to End Homelessness
www.endhomelessness.org

The Nature Conservancy
www.nature.org

Oxfam International
www.oxfam.org

United Way
www.unitedway.org

What Kids Can Do
www.whatkidscando.com

Wildlife Conservation Society
www.wcs.org

World Vision
www.worldvision.org

www.heifer.org

CELEBRATE!

When you finish a project, take time to celebrate a job well done! Have a pizza party, go swimming, play music, or do something else just for fun. Then gather together to admire your work, talk about what went well, and make plans for future projects. Share what you accomplished with others, too. Maybe they would like to join up to help, and they might have new ideas of what your group can do together. Most of all, be proud that you have made a difference!

INDEX

More Good Children's Books from Williamson Books

Williamson Books are available from your bookseller or directly from Ideals Publications. Please see last page for ordering information or to visit our website.

Also by Rebecca Olien

KIDS WRITE!
Fantasy & Sci Fi, Mystery, Autobiography, Adventure & More!

Full Color

AWESOME OCEAN SCIENCE
Investigating the Secrets of the Underwater World
by Cindy A. Littlefield

SUPER SCIENCE CONCOCTIONS
50 Mysterious Mixtures for Fabulous Fun
by Jill Frankel Hauser

BECOMING THE BEST YOU CAN BE!
Developing 5 Traits You Need
to Achieve Your Personal Best
by Jill Frankel Hauser

LIGHTHOUSES OF NORTH AMERICA!
Exploring Their History, Lore & Science
by Lisa Trumbauer

TALES ALIVE!
Ten Multicultural Folktales with Activities
by Susan Milord

American Bookseller Pick of the Lists
Skipping Stones Nature & Ecology Honor Award
ECOART!
Earth-Friendly Art & Craft Experiences
for 3- to 9-Year-Olds
by Laurie Carlson

Learning Magazine Teachers' Choice Award
KIDS' EASY-TO-CREATE WILDLIFE HABITATS
For Small Spaces in City, Suburb, Countryside
by Emily Stetson

Parents' Choice Gold Award
Dr. Toy Best Vacation Product
THE KIDS' NATURE BOOK
365 Indoor/Outdoor Activities & Experiences
by Susan Milord

Skipping Stones Nature & Ecology Honor Award
Parents' Choice Honor Award
The National Parenting Center Seal of Approval Award
MONARCH MAGIC
Butterfly Activities & Nature Discoveries
by Lynn M. Rosenblatt

Full Color

Parents' Choice Recommended
THE KIDS' BOOK OF WEATHER FORECASTING
Build a Weather Station, "Read" the Sky
& Make Predictions!
by Mark Breen & Kathleen Friestad

Children's Digest Health Education Award
Parents' Choice Recommended
ForeWord Magazine Book of the Year Honorable Mention
THE KIDS' GUIDE TO FIRST AID
All about Bruises, Burns, Stings,
Sprains & Other Ouches
by Karen Buhler Gale, R.N.

Parents' Choice Gold Award
American Bookseller Pick of the Lists
THE KIDS' MULTICULTURAL ART BOOK
Art & Craft Experiences from Around the World
by Alexandra M. Terzian

American Bookseller Pick of the Lists
Dr. Toy Best Vacation Product
KIDS' CRAZY ART CONCOCTIONS
50 Mysterious Mixtures for Art & Craft Fun
by Jill Frankel Hauser

American Bookseller Pick of the Lists
Parents' Choice Recommended
ADVENTURES IN ART
Arts & Crafts Experiences for 8- to 13-Year-Olds
by Susan Milord

THE KIDS' MULTICULTURAL CRAFT BOOK
35 Crafts from Around the World
by Roberta Gould

WORDPLAY CAFÉ
Cool Codes, Priceless Puzzles &
Phantastic Phonetic Phun
by Michael Kline

GREAT GAMES!
Ball, Board, Quiz & Word,
Indoors & Out, for Many or Few!
by Sam Taggar with Susan Williamson

Full Color

KIDS MAKE MAGIC
The complete Guide to
Becoming an Amazing Magician
by Ron Burgess

ForeWord Magazine Book of the Year Gold Award
THE SECRET LIFE OF MATH
Discover How (and Why) Numbers Have
Survived from the Cave Dwellers to Us!
by Ann McCallum

American Bookseller Pick of the Lists
Benjamin Franklin Best Education/Teaching Award
American Institute of Physics Science Writing Award
Parents' Choice Honor Award

GIZMOS & GADGETS
Creating Science Contraptions
that Work (& Knowing Why)
by Jill Frankel Hauser

Learning Magazine Teachers' Choice Award
GEOLOGY ROCKS!
50 Hands-on Activities to Explore the Earth
by Cindy Blobaum

ForeWord Magazine Book of the Year Finalist
SKYSCRAPERS!
Super Structures to Design & Build
by Carol A. Johmann

Parents' Choice Recommended
BRIDGES!
Amazing Structures to Design, Build & Test
by Carol A. Johmann & Elizabeth J. Reith

Parents' Choice Silver Honor Award
ANCIENT ROME!
Exploring the Culture, People & Ideas
of this Powerful Empire
by Avery Hart & Sandra Gallagher

Benjamin Franklin Silver Award
GOING WEST!
Journey on a Wagon Train to Settle a Frontier Town
by Carol A. Johmann & Elizabeth J. Reith

Children's Book Council Notable Book
American Bookseller Pick of the Lists
Dr. Toy 10 Best Education Products
PYRAMIDS!
50 Hands-on Activities to Experience Ancient Egypt
by Avery Hart & Paul Mantell

American Bookseller Pick of the Lists
MEXICO!
40 Activities to Experience Mexico Past & Present
by Susan Milord

American Bookseller Pick of the Lists
Parent's Guide Children's Media Award
ANCIENT GREECE!
40 Hands-on Activities to Experience
this Wondrous Age
by Avery Hart & Paul Mantell

Parents' Choice Silver Honor Award
THE LEWIS & CLARK EXPEDITION
Join the Corps of Discovery to Explore Uncharted Territory
by Carol A. Johmann

Children's Book Council Notable Book
American Bookseller Pick of the Lists
Dr. Toy 100 Best Children's Products
KNIGHTS & CASTLES
50 Hands-on Activities to Experience the Middle Ages
by Avery Hart & Paul Mantell

VISIT OUR WEBSITE!
To see what's new with Williamson Books and Ideals
Publications and learn more about specific titles, visit
our website at: **www.idealsbooks.com**

To Order Books:
You'll find Williamson Books at your favorite book-
store or you can order directly from Ideals
Publications. We accept Visa and MasterCard
(please include the number and expiration date).

Order on our secure website:
www.idealsbooks.com

Toll-free phone orders with credit cards:
1-800-586-2572

Toll-free fax orders:
1-888-815-2759

Or send a check with your order to:
Ideals Publications
Williamson Books Orders
535 Metroplex Drive, Suite 250
Nashville, Tennessee 37211

Catalog request: web, mail, or phone

Please add **$4.00** for postage for one book plus **$1.00**
for each additional book. Satisfaction is guaranteed
or full refund without questions or quibbles.